"*Claim Your Crown* speaks to the truth of who we really are. I believe the key to unlocking joy, purpose, and peace is discovering what it means to be daughters of the King. This book will be a guide to walk you through that journey!"

Kristen Dalton Wolfe, bestselling author of *The Sparkle Effect*, founder of She Is More, and former Miss USA

"Tarah-Lynn does a beautiful job of speaking directly to women like they are her sistas. She holds nothing back from telling radical truths in a way that invites us to claim our royal positions as daughters of the King. While reading these words, I was inspired and empowered to have more conversations with Jesus and encouraged to share the love that I've received with others!"

Chelsea Hurst, cohost of the *Encounter Now* podcast and author of *Above All Else*

Claim Your Crown

Cierra, you are
indeed a daughter
of the King.
Love you to life

-Carissa

Dec 2020

Walking in

CONFIDENCE AND WORTH

as a Daughter of the King

TARAH-LYNN SAINT-ELIEN

a division of Baker Publishing Group
Grand Rapids, Michigan

Published by Revell
a division of Baker Publishing Group
PO Box 6287, Grand Rapids, MI 49516-6287
www.revellbooks.com

Printed in the United States of America

Library of Congress Cataloging-in-Publication Data
Names: Saint-Elien, Tarah-Lynn, author.
Title: Claim your crown : walking in confidence and worth as a daughter of the king / Tarah-Lynn Saint-Elien.
Description: Grand Rapids, Michigan : Revell, a division of Baker Publishing Group, 2019. | Includes bibliographical references.
Identifiers: LCCN 2019039578 | ISBN 9780800736958
Subjects: LCSH: Christian women—Religious life. | Identity (Psychology)—Religious aspects—Christianity. | Self-confidence—Religious aspects—Christianity.
Classification: LCC BV4527 .S225 2019 | DDC 248.8/43—dc23
LC record available at https://lccn.loc.gov/2019039578

The Proprietor is represented by the literary agency of Credo Communications, LLC, Grand Rapids, Michigan, www.credocommunications.net.

In keeping with biblical principles of creation stewardship, Baker Publishing Group advocates the responsible use of our natural resources. As a member of the Green Press Initiative, our company uses recycled paper when possible. The text paper of this book is composed in part of post-consumer waste.

20 21 22 23 24 25 26 7 6 5 4 3 2 1

To God, who adorned me with my crown first.

Mommy—the queen of my heart,
Pops and Mitch—the kings of my world,
Medgina and Shermine—my forever sister queens:
I'm honored to live, laugh, and rule by your sides.

And to you, my beautiful readers:
Let's claim our crowns together.

Contents

Foreword

When I walked into the party, everybody just stopped.

I wrote these lyrics as the first line to my song "Party Like a Princess," but truthfully it was much more than a song. It was the recap of my entrance to my high school spring formal, prom, and every college dance I attended.

Even the DJ wasn't ready to see me without
A boy who isn't ready to be a king—
So tell me, why would I be chasing him to be his queen?

The lyrics told the story of every red carpet from the Grammys to the Dove Awards and even my Instagram feed and snaps on Snapchat. From my teen years to my midtwenties, I was somewhat known for never showing up to events with or sharing social media posts of a boyfriend or a boy friend, and this song was essentially the reason why.

Don't you know who my Daddy is?
Don't you know what my Daddy did?

Don't you know who my Daddy is?
He paid it all—I'm the belle of this ball.

I was frustrated that my singlehood seemed to be synonymous with sadness or loneliness. There were definitely moments of frustration and wanting to be in love when I wasn't, but ultimately, I found my hope in a relationship much greater than what any guy could ever give me. Though I went on a few dates here and there throughout college and my early twenties, and truly desired to be a wife, I never wanted my worth or value to be defined by a relationship status. I never wanted to give in to the pressure to have a guy on my arm or in a photo with me—as if that was the key to finding joy and defining who I was. I prayed diligently for my future husband, knowing that he would be worth waiting for, while also choosing to celebrate the season of being single.

I don't need a prince to party like a princess.

In the spring of 2018, I married the love of my life. Aaron is my best friend, my road trip partner, my forever date, and the father of our incredible daughter, Isabella. He makes me laugh more than anyone I've ever met and always knows what I want to eat when I can't make up my mind. Even so, he is *not* the source of my worth or value.

I find my worth in God and God alone. I find my value in knowing that I was created by Him and for Him. He made the skies, seas, and all things beautiful—including each one of us. *Including you.* When He looks at us, He sees His daughters—and as He is the King of all kings, that makes us princesses.

The title *princess* can often seem like it's reserved for movie characters and international royalty, but it's available to us too. By breathing in, breathing out, and acknowledging life, we are accepting the gift of being a daughter of the King. And *that* is a reason to celebrate.

Tarah-Lynn knows and lives this message well. She is not only confident in who she is as a daughter of the King, she literally rocks a crown in real life too! But whether you believe you deserve a crown or not, whether you're single, married, young, or old, you *are* royalty. You deserve to know that you have a seat at a table set for the King, and this book will take you on that journey so you can claim your crown.

Jamie Grace, actress, podcaster,
and award-winning singer-songwriter

Introduction

So, there's this guy. . . . The best love stories begin with this, don't they?

Anyway.

Okay, girl, so He's definitely your type. Whenever He walks into the room, He owns it. He's always in control . . . but not in a controlling way. He pays attention to the slightest details and is fiercely protective—not overbearing or anything. He's gentle with all and has a reassuring peace about Him. And oh, how He loves? Swoon.

This One's different. He's been waiting on the day you'd give Him a proper chance.

He writes you love letters that are signed with His name at the bottom, but you sometimes return to sender. He looks out for you, but you'll often call it luck. He has a whole love story written out for you, but you've been known to call it a fairy tale.

I'm going to be real with you. Maybe the world has told you otherwise, but He has put it on my heart to reverse your thinking, to erase how you perceive yourself.

You are a queen. Or princess—whatever suits your fancy. God wants you to experience His love, and He wants you to know that as His daughter, you are indeed royalty.

As little girls, we may have been infatuated with princesses, but I find we've become disillusioned in a way that's detrimental to our self-awareness. Not many of us women are conscious of our own crowns.

We go through life seeking validation from our peers, our family, the media, men—it's a never-ending cycle. We see other women as competition. We stand awestruck at celebrities, picking out the physical traits we wish we could replace on our own bodies. We speak lowly of ourselves, dashing outright opportunities that could propel us forward. We say we don't want to be alone, and so we look for love in the wrong places. We go from heartbreak to heartbreak, blaming ourselves when the issue has never been us.

It has always been the distorted mirror.

When the crown was placed on my head and I was titled Miss Black New Jersey 2018, my perspective of being a queen changed. Having more opportunities to travel and talk to young women and girls in my home state and overseas made me experience what being a queen entailed. Seeing their lingering gaze on my crown made me desperately want to show all women the crowns they already have.

I've been doing so through my blog, *Adorned in Armor*—a place where I encourage women to conquer life through faith and fashion. I truly believe it is imperative for every woman to realize her worth in order to flourish in life, and I illustrate this through style posts and personal stories. However, I knew the most effective way to share lessons of queendom was through a book. *This* book.

And so, here I am.

Claim Your Crown is for you. It's an inspirational guide for young women who are deeply dissatisfied with society's standards and desire more for themselves. In learning to view God as a loving Father and King of all kings, you will discover your immeasurable worth as well as the power you have simply by being who you are. You will come to understand that your crown has *always* existed—without a prince—and you'll discover how to properly dismiss distractions in order to confidently reign.

As you journey through this book, you'll also grow spiritually—swapping society's teachings for biblical principles and establishing a strong foundation in positive self-worth. You will begin to see yourself the way God sees you: as an heiress of the kingdom. You will learn to claim your inheritance and independence. You'll find a desire churning within you to mirror positive examples of women in the Bible, discover the righteous response to dealing with your battles, and walk in the light of authority.

Claim Your Crown thwarts the media's misconceptions about beauty and womanhood while teaching God's original intent. It delves into the recurrent insecurities, fears, doubts, and guilt young women face daily. Most are things that I've dealt with myself.

You'll find me keeping it real with you as if I'm one of your girls (because I am) by sharing my own personal anecdotes, popular culture (I mean, I *am* a millennial), and fairy tales as organizing principles (because let's face it, a girl still dreams). You'll explore God's reign and the power we all have as His daughters. Not only will we relate to one another, we'll also find real connections to the women in the Bible.

Every chapter will refresh you with biblically based encouragement, empowering you not only to claim the promises of God but also to walk purposefully in them.

I'm ecstatic to bring you along on this voyage of yanking back the authority from outside forces and redirecting that power to falling in love with your true self. I can't wait to hear of the new ways in which you experience the love of God and embrace your God-given crown!

I'm telling you, He adores you. That Guy I was telling you about earlier, I mean. He knew you before you were even conceived. He positioned the stars in the vast skies, and still, He knows you by your name. He even knows your heart. He came to earth, got lash after lash—physically, verbally—He took it all just for you. He willingly gave Himself up to die for you. That's how beautiful He thinks you are. That's how worth it He knows you are. He thought you were to die for.

This "Guy"—this Jesus—wants you to come to know your worth too. As you venture through *Claim Your Crown*, you'll feel the love of God ricocheting off the pages and knocking at your heart. It is my prayer that you glean this insight, zealous to pay it forward by helping guide other princesses and queens in your life.

I see it now: you, standing taller—your crown glistening and shining in every passing reflection. I feel that fire burning within you as you thumb through the pages in anticipation, plotting your reign. I see you owning life the way a real queen should—boldly navigating life as the royal you are.

One

A ROYAL REALITY

The best princess movie of all time is *Cinderella*—the Brandy and Whitney Houston version, of course. If you disagree, let's talk this out. And if you don't know it (*gasp*), this is your cue to move your little cursor right over, open a tab for YouTube, and watch right now. No, think of it as a treat after you finish this book.

As kids, my siblings and I would pop the tape into our VCR (it was the early 2000s, y'all) and prance around our basement, stepping on one another's toes as if we were at the ball. We'd reenact the hilarious scenes of the evil stepsisters trying to stuff themselves into their two-sizes-too-small dresses. And to this day, my siblings and I randomly belt out "Impossible!" in our best Brandy and Whitney Houston voices.

Aside from the beautiful wardrobe and catchy songs, there was something about the film that made it appealing and relatable. I mean, who else sang "In My Own Little Corner" while doing chores?

Prior to movies like Brandy's *Cinderella*, the world primarily saw royalty depicted in England's Queen Elizabeth, picture books, and animated cartoons. Being a royal wasn't intended for us commoners. So I suppose seeing Cinderella come to life made princesses more relatable for me.

We can all see why the modern fairy tale of Meghan Markle and Prince Harry captivated everyone around the world. And on the day of the royal wedding, the world watched along either in awe, indifference, or disgust due to her race.

I, of course, was in full support of Meghan's major come up. I was equally fascinated with the hilarious memes about her impending rule and, on a serious note, the "implications" of including a woman of color into the royal family.

Meghan faced tons of backlash simply for being Black; she was judged for her familial background and for being a divorcée. She will continue to experience even more scrutiny as a royal. Though some saw her as unsuitable for the throne, it was simply meant to be.

Understandably, there was even a focus on her title when the big fairy-tale wedding was approaching. The conversation made clear that if Prince Harry should marry Meghan, she wouldn't officially have the princess title along her own name. She doesn't have that right. "Princess Meghan" couldn't even be a thing; she would be called Her Royal Highness Princess *Harry* of Wales. Harry—not Meghan.

Not only that, it is tradition that the queen bestows the honors, so should Queen Elizabeth II decide to make her grandson a duke the day of the wedding, Meghan would become either Her Royal Highness Princess Harry of Wales *or* Her Royal Highness the Duchess of Sussex. We now know she's the latter! (Fun fact: She is actually the first woman to be known as such.)

The Duke and Duchess of Sussex drove the belief that dreams do come true and that fairy-tale endings could happen for *any*body. It reminded me of childhood.

Growing up, our lives as royals weren't for pretend in my home. My parents made it a reality for my siblings and me. We were brought up knowing we must carry ourselves with dignity and respect. We were taught to know our worth. We were raised as princes and princesses. In fact, my nickname was (and maybe kinda still is) "Princess."

Yes, the title came about as a form of endearment. However, I didn't just receive the crown for being a girl . . . or for being the firstborn. Being called Princess is packed with meaning primarily because my heavenly Father's a King. And as one of God's own, you are a royal too.

Yes, you.

We tiptoe through life as if we are Cinderella past midnight. Our carriages? Mere pumpkins. Our glass slippers? An illusion to disguise our bare feet. With shards of glass stuck on our past, we're cut so deeply and can't see hope for the future.

But what would your life look like if you truly believed—you *are* royalty?

I recently came across an article relating a new discovery about Disney princesses. Cinderella, Tiana, and Belle—the ones who married into royalty—wore opera gloves. Those born royal, however, didn't. Think Snow White, Aurora, and Ariel. They are elegantly adorned by their bare hands.[1]

Okay. Now, bear with me; I'm putting on my English minor cap for this one. It seems that the princesses who wore gloves represent an untouchable aristocracy and society's view of their unworthiness to be accepted as they are. Here's my message to you: the world may be reluctant to see your crown, but God is ever so accepting of you.

You, queen, are automatically deemed royalty as a child of God. You were born with royal blood. You are crowned with glory and honor; you have dominion over all (Ps. 8:5).

What you are called doesn't depend on the names others bestow upon you. You don't have to marry into a royal family to be royal. You don't have to worry about how you are perceived in the public eye. People will try to disqualify you, but there has always been a crown with your name on it.

There is no official title needed other than child of the Creator of the universe.

Your right to the throne isn't just happenstance. You are *chosen*. The Passion Translation of 1 Peter 2:9 tells us, "But you are God's chosen treasure—priests who are kings, a spiritual 'nation' set apart as God's devoted ones. He called you out of darkness to experience his marvelous light, and now he claims you as his very own. He did this so that you would broadcast his glorious wonders throughout the world."

You are *His very own*. How can we wrap our minds around the fact that our Father is our King? It's hard to grasp, but it is a reality. *Our* royal reality. Now, own it.

Kingdom Keys

- What you are called isn't dependent on the names others decide to bestow upon you. You don't have to marry into a royal family to be royal. You don't have to worry about how you are perceived in the public eye. People will try to disqualify you, but there has always been a crown with your name on it. There is no official title needed other than child of the Creator of the universe.

- Your Father is the King of all kings. He chose you; you are God's very own.

Reflection: *We've discussed the proof of your royal status but what about your emotions? Do you feel you belong in the royal family of God? If not, who or what caused you to feel you don't?*

OUR KING

When you think of God's splendor, what words do you use to describe Him? There are countless ways to describe God, but I decided to stick to five major themes.

God Is Omnipotent

Due to the fact I'm an extreme advocate for the color pink and high heels, people are often shocked when I say I'm into superhero films. And though I don't necessarily have a favorite, I'm particularly drawn to Superman and Thor for their mega strength. I'm in awe of their ability to toss cars left and right and how they can be attacked yet remain unaffected.

They all have weaknesses, however, don't they? For Superman, it's kryptonite, and for Thor, it's his reliance on his hammer. If Superman is pierced with the radioactive product, he's pretty much a goner. Should Thor be without his hammer for a few seconds, he faces the same fate.

With us, we don't have to worry about how the superhero will come out on top in our lives because (spoiler) we have the victory over the enemy thanks to Christ Jesus. God is the King of Kings and always wins.

The characters we know and love are *almost* invincible. Almost. However, our God is totally invincible. He is omnipotent, meaning He is *all* powerful. Not a little, not some, but all. God has no weakness, no limitations. His strength is absolute. He controls all of earth's elements and can defy gravity. He can do anything and everything with His infinite power.

Not only does God hold the whole world in His hands, but His power also gives us hope. Because He is in control, we can remain confident and grow into who He has called us to be. It is through His power that we can flourish and live our best lives (John 10:10). It is through His power that we are transformed into royal beings.

God Is Omniscient

God is omniscient, or all-knowing. As a child, I occasionally imagined God smiting me for creating outlandish scenarios in my mind.

Allow me to take you back to Tarah-land circa 2006-ish. We had just finished the congregational prayer, but for some reason, preteen Tarah is still kneeling. Shifting her weight from one knee to the other, she pulls two dollars out of her tiny purse, and with her elbows firmly planted on the pew, she begins to wriggle the bills around. She had plans to give one dollar to God and save the other for buying snacks after church.

But right as the offering basket came around, someone's grandmother stood over her, snatched the bills out of both hands, and tossed them into the basket.

Preteen Tarah wanted to dive for the basket but, of course, she didn't. Instead, she imagined things that would give the *Mean Girls* a run for their money.

Then she remembered that God could hear her thoughts . . . and that she was in church. Borderline fearing for her life (I'm totally kidding), she was like, "Oh snap, girl, you gotta stop."

She didn't think God would smite her outright—she thought of her punishment as one from those humorous television shows where a cartoon character is minding their business and is zapped from the heavens.

Today, I now love that God knows what I'm thinking. It allows me to keep it real with Him. I can't keep a secret from Him, so why not share with Him?

Think about it.

His omniscience also comforts me when I'm going through tough times and I haven't a clue what to say in prayer. You know those nights when you're burying your hiccupped sobs into your pillows? He knows what your hurt is saying.

> The Holy Spirit takes hold of us in our human frailty to empower us in our weakness. For example, at times we don't even know how to pray, or know the best things to ask for. But the Holy Spirit rises up within us to super-intercede on our behalf, pleading to God with emotional sighs too deep for words.

> God, the searcher of the heart, knows our longings, yet he also understands the desires of the Spirit, because the Holy Spirit passionately pleads before God for us, his holy ones, in perfect harmony with God's plan and our destiny. (Rom. 8:26–27 TPT)

Isn't it comforting to know that God sent us a powerful Helper, especially for the times we don't know what we need? The Spirit swoops in to rescue the words lodged in our throats from the ache we feel. God searches our hearts and knows what we need, and He is there.

He knows what's stopping you from claiming your crown. He knows your insecurities, your doubts. He knows the answers to your hardest assignments. He knows why that man broke your heart. He knows why your boss fired you. He knows it all because, big or small, He is into the details. He is an intricate God and is working in every piece of your life.

Your binoculars may bear the image of thunderous waves ahead, but you can trust that God is at the helm, navigating your ship. Even when the storms of life threaten to overtake you—He won't let them wreck you. He won't let you sink.

Romans 8:28 tells us, "And we know that God causes everything to work together for the good of those who love God and are called according to his purpose for them."

That's why it's imperative to be on the same page with Him. Though we don't know what comes next, God can and will prepare us as we listen to Him. When we know the Bible for ourselves and we're open with God, we'll find ourselves *in tune* with Him, no matter where life takes us.

Nothing can catch God by surprise because He knows the past, present, and future. He lives in eternity and is waiting for us there. It's time we take every step with Him as we're on our way to walking in the authority He has already given us.

God Is Omnipresent

God is omnipresent, or everywhere all at once. "'Who can hide in secret places so that I cannot see them?' declares the LORD. 'Do not I fill heaven and earth?' declares the LORD" (Jer. 23:24 NIV).

Absolutely nothing and no one can be hidden from Him. According to Hebrews 4:13, "Everything is uncovered and exposed for Him to see. We must answer to Him" (GW). In other words, whatever we think we do in private is actually public because God has a full, clear view. We are accountable for all we do.

God Is Love

I always chuckle whenever I hear the phrase "God is love." I think of MTV's *Run's House*—probably the only show my parents deemed suitable for me to watch on the network as a teenager.

My sisters and I enjoyed watching the huge Simmons family and all of their shenanigans. I remember the adventures the siblings would have—their amusing bickering, the love they shared, and the lessons they learned. At the end of every episode, Rev Run DMC would run a bath, share some thoughts, and then finally say "God is love" as the screen faded to black.

But what does "God is love" really mean?

God is love because:

- God is the ultimate source. He created the world and everything in it; love begins and ends with Him. His greatest commandment is to love Him and one another. It is also our delight and joy to be His light and show love to the world.
- God made the ultimate sacrifice. All people have sinned and fallen short of God's principle (Rom. 3:23), and there is a huge space—a chasm—between God and us. We have no way to overcome that gulf on our own. But the greatest act of love in history was demonstrated when God sent His one and only son, Christ Jesus, to live on earth and to die for our sins. In doing this, Christ bridged the gap that existed between God and us and brought us close to His side. It is through Christ that we can reach our pure and holy Father. He sent His *own son* to rescue *us* from eternal damnation. So now, we can experience Christ's love every single day! Yes, He loves us *that* much.
- When we believe in the death and resurrection of Christ, God begins to work in our hearts. He shows us grace and changes us from the inside out. First John 3:1 tells us, "See what great love the Father has lavished on us, that we should be called children of God! And that is what we are! The reason the world does not know us is that it did not know him" (NIV).

Okay, whew. That got deep pretty quick. It was all necessary, however, considering I didn't always see God as a loving

Father. I saw Him as a tense Judge—a King waiting to punish us little peasants whenever we misbehaved.

However, since I was a little girl, seeing my mother's love for God showed me the existence of His love. She has been sick for about eighteen years now—practically, my entire life. She was diagnosed with avascular necrosis when doctors found her femur bones rotted black. She has had over eight unsuccessful surgeries, and the growing bones in her thighs grind against the artificial bones, causing her constant pain and a walking disability. Most recently, she suffered from an unrelated stroke that led to a speech impediment and memory loss. Her body is constantly in agony; however, Christ is her joy.

People see her strength and ask her versions of "You're so young and you're suffering like this—how do you stay so happy? How do you maintain a positive spirit?"

My queen's answer is always Jesus.

This isn't just a name she says. This is the Name above *all* names. This is the Name by which she lives her life. Witnessing her praise throughout my childhood provided evidence God's love was there. I'm especially in awe of her ability to provide encouragement, to pray powerful prayers, and to carry the weight of others' hurts and burdens.

Growing up, I always ran to my mother when I was in pain. Today, I still do—*however*, she gets upset when I'm not happy, so I no longer bring her every single trouble. I don't want her to carry it all. As I've gotten older, I've become more aware of her pain and her own limitations. Therefore, I run to God for her too.

God has shown me His love through my mother's suffering, but it wasn't until my own personal heartbreak that I truly experienced His love. I've gone from spilling all my problems to Mom to dragging them all to God and leaving them there.

Though I've lived only twenty-three years, I've discovered there's nothing on earth like a mother's love and concern. Absolutely nothing.

God's embraces are quite literally out of this world, however. You can pour out everything to Him. God caresses your heart and ministers to your wounds. He reminds you that you'll be okay, and He reaffirms His love for you.

The greatness of God is truly indescribable. So far, we've only scratched the surface. He is love . . . and surely, He is King.

God Is King

> Greatness, power, splendor, glory, and majesty are yours, Lord, because everything in heaven and on earth is yours. The kingdom is yours, Lord, and you are honored as head of all things. Riches and honor are in front of you. You rule everything. You hold power and strength in your hands, and you can make anyone great and strong. (1 Chron. 29:11–12 GW)

We know the world never loved Christ, so undoubtedly, there will be attacks on the church. Revelation 17:14 tells us how the rulers of the world are positioned against Jesus. However, the reality is that no force can come against our Father. Though there are many who wage war against Christ, 1 Corinthians 15:25 reminds us that they can't ever win because they are under His feet. Because God reigns over all, He will forever be victorious. That makes us more than conquerors, queen! And it gets even better: there will be a day when every single knee will bow to Him (Phil. 2:9–11).

Jesus is alive, sitting at the right hand of the Father, and will rule forever and ever (Exod. 15:18). Knowing your Father is a King who will never lose—knowing His invincibility and love—will make you confident in whose you are.

- God's power is absolute; He has no weakness.
- God is omniscient and omnipresent.
- When we don't know what to say or pray in tough times, the Holy Spirit swoops in to rescue the words lodged in our throats from the ache we feel.

- God isn't a cruel ruler waiting to punish us as peasants. Our King is love.

Reflection: *What is your weakness? How does God's strength show up in your life?*

HEIRESS

Who are you?

Naturally, you probably thought of your name. Perhaps you went a bit further and started referring to your characteristics. That's cool and all, but . . .

Do you truly know who you are in Christ?

Genesis 1:26 lets us know we were made in the image of God. In other words, when God created humankind, He formed us as a copy of Himself. We are meant to serve as the tangible representation of who our Creator is.

Maybe you're thinking, *I'm flawed. I make mistakes all the time. I am not perfect or anywhere remotely close to who God is.* #True. You're completely right. We fall short by a landslide. Mudslide. Yup, all of that.

However, when Adam and Eve disobeyed God and bit into the forbidden fruit, their disobedience did not change the fact they were made in God's image. No, sin only disfigured it.

Because we are fallen beings, we are qualified for redemption. What I love about blemishes and messes is that they can be healed, perfected, and made clean. Christ did that. He wiped the ugliness right up and is in the business of renewal—over and over again.

Shout out to our Big Brother, right?

No, I'm not referring to a dystopian (and weird) book we were required to read in high school English class. I'm still talking about Jesus. His sacrifice gave us the honor of being adopted into the royal family. We all are God's creation, but in receiving Jesus, we become God's children.

> And you did not receive the "spirit of religious duty," leading you back into the fear of never being good enough. But you have received the "Spirit of full acceptance," enfolding you into the family of God. And you will never feel orphaned, for as he rises up within us, our spirits join him in saying the words of tender affection, "Beloved Father!" (Rom. 8:15 TPT)

I don't know what your life looks like. I don't know whether your mother or father is in the picture. I don't know if your bond with them is strong or if it is strained. What I do know is you are not an orphan. You are not alone. You are not cut off from the family tree. You have a good, good Father, and you are loved by Him! (I would be remiss if I didn't reference that song at that moment.)

How blessed are we to be able to call God "Father"?

How blessed are we to have access to comfort, joy, and freedom?

How blessed are we to be heiresses of the kingdom?

How blessed are we to be chosen?

How blessed are we to be rich?

Though I truly believe God has called each one of His children to live fruitful lives, the richness I'm currently referring to is our reward in heaven. There's a fullness of life that brims over in the hands of the Father. Romans 8:17 tells us, "Since we are his children, we are his heirs."

An heiress is defined as a woman who inherits huge sums of money, a title, and/or property. She's basically the girl who gets the goods when the family member ahead of her dies. There's absolutely no way for an heir to obtain the fortune until this happens.

And, it did.

Christ died for you to give you *abundant* life. You have life here on earth and can look forward to living again on the other side of eternity.

When Drake's hit single "The Motto" was released, many of my peers adopted the "YOLO" (You Only Live Once) mantra with abandon. The song almost gave people an excuse to do the most daring things in all shapes and forms. Though the song is now old news, many of us still live to the extreme—either unaware that we're doing it or dismissive of the fact that there are repercussions in this life and the next for making bad choices.

Sis, we must adopt a new mantra. We live not once but *twice*. And how we choose to live in this life determines our final destination. It's time we choose heaven, not just with our lips but with our lives.

Heaven will be indescribable. And God is so good that He doesn't want us to wait until we get there to live our best lives.

He wants us to live our lives to the fullest now! It is possible to have a good time outside of what the world glorifies.

Dream big. Do what makes your heart happy (and pleases God). Go on that trip with your girls or go solo. Lavish yourself in love. Go for the very bewildering opportunity you have no option but to believe in God for.

As a King's kid, you have the audacity to claim your inheritance and all God has promised to you. When you choose to belong to Christ, you become an heiress (Rom. 8:17) and receive all the promises reserved for Abraham's descendants (Gal. 3:29).

God sent the Holy Spirit to seal the deal on the inheritance He promised (Eph. 1:13–14). When we believe Christ and become His followers, we also must seek to live in His will. I'm finding that the best way to do this is by first learning to trust in God and to believe in His promises—no matter what our circumstances look like.

Blessings beyond Our Belief

The unique blessings God bestows upon our lives are *ours*, but we won't experience the fullness of them here on earth if we're filled with doubt.

You want to know someone who had trouble trusting God? Abraham's wife, Sarah. Yes, *that* Abraham, the same man God chose to be the father of all nations. In Genesis 18:18, God promised Abraham that he would undoubtedly become "a great and powerful nation, and all nations on earth will be blessed through him" (NIV). (That's us, girl!)

God loved him, and Abraham was extremely faithful to God. Abraham was the epitome of "ride or die" back then. How ironic is it that as years passed, both he and his wife lacked faith in what God said?

Sarah couldn't see the promise because she was staring at her glaring circumstances. God had promised nations and blessings, but here they were, old and barren, when, in order to be blessed, the nations would have to be of their lineage.

Then comes one of my favorite parts in the Bible—I promise, I'm going somewhere with this. Sarah laughed when it was prophesied that she would have a baby in her old age. The Lord talked to Abraham like, "Did your girl just laugh at me?" Shaken, Sarah said no. God replied with, "Yes, you did."

He punk'd her! Our God has a sense of humor, in case you didn't know.

Like Sarah, we will struggle with trusting in what God says, but no matter what we feel or think, His promises always show themselves true. (I mean, we're Abraham's spiritual descendants here today!) Whether you believe it or not, the promise is yours. Place all of your assets into the trust of God; your fund will be found there.

I know how you feel, girl. This isn't easy. Quite recently, I found I don't trust God myself. Not in the ways I should. He has shown me this in multiple ways, but the most mind-blowing example was what He revealed to me when I was struggling to choose my "word of the year" in the beginning of 2018.

In late February, I attended a fashion and beauty conference and went home with a gigantic bag of goods from many sponsors. There were tons of makeup and beauty products, books, fashion boxes, and sunglasses for days. There was also a jewelry box that I was especially drawn to. I opened it to find a tiny, iridescent bracelet with the word *believe* glinting back at me.

I find that word pretty . . . regular. *Believe* is the word you find on every girl's dorm room poster and in the kitchens and hallways of every young woman's apartment. It isn't a "special" word.

However, I still looked at the bracelet thinking, *Hmm, ah okay, I'll just wear this as a reminder to believe in God's promises*. Because, yes, I'm the type of girl who assigns meaning to precious items.

The next morning, I opened up my Bible to read. The youth group I lead at my church was going through a "New Testament in a Year" Bible reading plan. We were in the book of Acts then and as I was venturing into whatever chapter that was, the metals of my bracelet lit up against the page, leaving soft colors of pinks, yellows, and blues. I paused my reading and glimpsed at it. Toying with its shimmery stones, I noticed a circular pendant that lay adjacent to the word *believe*. It glided and lay softly as I highlighted and flipped through the pages.

Looking closer, I noticed the pendant for the second time. There was a code on it: A0942. I did notice it upon first opening the box but merely considered it just a cluster of random numbers used by manufacturers to keep track of inventory. This time, I didn't think of it as such.

Because I was in the book of Acts, my mind immediately referred back to Scripture. Was there an Acts 9:42?

Yes!

I flipped a few pages back and landed on the verse. Acts 9:42 said, "The news spread through the whole town, and many *believed* in the Lord" (emphasis added).

Okay, whoa, I thought. Believe *is in that verse!*

I looked at my bracelet a little bewildered and awed at the same time. Is this a Christian company?! I reached for the box and googled them. They weren't.

The company sells bracelets with words on each one—they use codes so that girls from all around the world can exchange them when they feel like the "word" has served its purpose.

God will go to great lengths and find intricate, special ways to speak to us. He wants us to increase our belief so He can reward us with more than what we can imagine.

The Scripture that brand referenced accidentally was what my God planned for me on purpose!

I went back to the Bible to read the chapter leading into the verse. You'll find that portion of the reading is when Saul, the biggest anti-Christian advocate, becomes a believer. However, the particular verse (Acts 9:42) follows the miracle of Peter resurrecting Tabitha, a selfless believer who was well-loved in her community.

This moment was pivotal not only because of the resurrecting power Peter received from Jesus but also because it inspired the early church and led to an influx of new believers! The miracle was so life-changing because it brought people to *believe* in the Truth.

Perhaps you're like Sarah and laugh at God's promises. Perhaps people laugh at you. Perhaps you are so blinded by a seemingly hopeless situation that you have no response.

Sis, we were not created to live like that!

Because we are God's children, we can dare to imagine. Because we are daughters of the Most High King, we can begin to see ourselves as heirs. Because we are kingdom kids, we have an inheritance in heaven and instant access to exceedingly abundantly more than all we ask or think—right here.

Put an end to the "perhaps" in your life and begin to believe in God's promises. Even when they seem crazy, God is proficient in the impossible.

We're told in the Passion Translation of Luke 11:13, "If imperfect parents know how to lovingly take care of their children and give them what they need, how much more will the perfect heavenly Father give the Holy Spirit's fullness when his children ask him."

As heiresses to the kingdom, we must confidently come to the throne. You are not a peasant—begging God for porridge is like praying for crumbs. Whether you pray with wild faith or faith the size of a mustard seed, God desires to present a feast to His princess.

Royal Protocol

We're blessed enough that we don't have to go through anyone to ask our King for anything. However, we still must come correctly to the throne. Let's call it royal protocol.

- Matthew 7:7 says, "Ask, and the gift is yours. Seek, and you'll discover. Knock, and the door will be opened for you" (TPT). What must we do? *Ask, seek, and knock* in order to receive from our Father.
- John 16:24 tells us we need to *ask in Jesus's name* and He'll grant us an overwhelming joy.
- John 14:13–14 says, "Whatever you ask in my name, this I will do, that the Father may be glorified in the

Son. If you ask me anything in my name, I will do it" (ESV). This may seem similar to the verses noted before, but there is a difference. Not only must we ask in Jesus's name, but the thing we're believing in God for *must also bring Him glory*. Is what you're asking for just for you or for the advancement of the kingdom?

- John 15:7 says, "If you abide in me, and my words abide in you, ask whatever you wish, and it will be done for you" (ESV). The only way we can abide in God is by knowing what He says in His Word, the Bible. Sure, we can ask what we want, but it must *align* with God's Word for Him to consider it for us.
- Finally, Matthew 21:22 says, "And whatever you ask in prayer, you will receive, if you have faith" (ESV).

"*If* you have faith."

If you believe.

I sometimes look at these verses and think, *Great, I can ask God for my wildest dreams and they will come to pass.*

But then life checks me. God is not only teaching me to be patient in His pauses; He is teaching me to listen for the answer He is trying to give me. He did not present a gospel of prosperity to us.

Indeed, God does want us to believe in all He can do through us. He has made promises that He will certainly keep, but there will be times when we don't get what we want—even when what we ask for honors Him. There will be times when He will gently tell us "no" or "wait." There will be times when we feel He hasn't answered at all. His response will always be out of love and for the betterment of our lives. Even when we can't see it yet, we must believe that, yes, our Father knows best.

Kingdom Keys

- We live not once but twice. How we choose to live in this life determines our final destination. Choose heaven not just with your lips but with your life.
- Approach the throne boldly.
- Sometimes, even when your request honors God, He may answer with a no.

Reflection: *In what ways can you begin to come out of your shell in your relationship with Christ?*

Four

ABDICATION

As a heavenly heiress, there are certain circumstances that simply do not apply to you. Take earthly heirs as an example. I'm talking kings . . . and presidents, even.

Many kings have been dethroned throughout history. How so? Murder. Revolts. Coups. Why? Wild tempers. Greed. Unpopularity. You catch my drift, right?

So many causes, all with the same result. Their thrones were taken from right under them, transporting these kings from cushioned seats to the butt of harsh reality. Their crowns revoked.

Imagine being kicked out of your own castle because your subjects simply didn't like you. Imagine your right to the throne susceptible to how people feel about you. Imagine the very people you trusted or people you have already known as traitors succeeding in dominating you. Surely, it's more complicated than that, but consider the gist of it all.

Shady. Shady. Sha-dy.

These overthrowings happened. And they still can, albeit in a more lawful, intricate, and drawn-out process. American presidents today still face the necessary threat of impeachment to keep them in check.

In hopes of going against the ingrained belief of there being a "perfect" president, Representative Elbridge Gerry of Massachusetts once said, "A good magistrate will not fear [impeachments]. A bad one ought to be kept in fear of them."[1]

Everyone—even the highest elected officials—can be dismissed.

Here on this earth, not everyone is fit to rule. Whether due to a myriad of mistakes or simply the wrong ambitions, they can be the rightful heir or justly elected and still lose their position.

That's not how the operation of the kingdom of God works.

Our King will not take back your crown just because He didn't care for your attitude. He will not swipe your crown right off your head because of horrendous decisions you made. He will not snatch back your crown because of that sin you're struggling with.

Isn't that a relief to know?

God will never revoke your title. Your position cannot be abdicated because it is His love that crowns you. No mistake or corrupted idea can keep you from God's mercy, grace, and compassion.

Grace. How often have we heard of it? It's a name parents call their children. It's a term church mothers have adopted in greeting when asked how they're doing. But really . . . what *is* it?

Grace is something you can't win over; it's something you can't work for. It's something God gives so freely and with abandon because He loves you. Grace is God's goodness and kindness toward us though we don't deserve it. The idea is unfathomable and immeasurable, but who wouldn't want to serve a limitless God?

> When God our Savior revealed his kindness and love, he saved us, not because of the righteous things we had done, but because of his mercy. He washed away our sins, giving us a new birth and new life through the Holy Spirit. He generously poured out the Spirit upon us through Jesus Christ our Savior. Because of his grace he made us right in his sight and gave us confidence that we will inherit eternal life. (Titus 3:4–7)

You don't have to do a thing! There is no striving. We all need to understand this, sis—it's vital. There's nothing you can say or do to make God love you more or love you less.

Yes, even that thing—you know the thing—*that* thing you refuse to let go. God is awaiting you to bring it to Him so He can fling it to the pits of hell. He wants to deliver you. He wants to set you free.

But you have to be able to loosen your own grip.

It's easier said than done, especially with the enemy in your ear. Satan cunningly replays your most mortifying moments in attempts to convince you, "You can't call yourself a Christian." He tells you, "You're a disgrace to God's family." He says, "You can't go back to God after this."

But you can. Call the enemy out for the liar that he is. God knows how you messed up, and He also knew of all the ways you would even before creation began. Yet, He still loves and chooses you (Eph. 1:4).

Grace is why we're still here. God doesn't get frustrated with us, nor does He await the perfect moment to punish us. Exodus 34:6–7 says He is "slow to anger and filled with unfailing love and faithfulness . . . lavish[ing] unfailing love to a thousand generations . . . [forgiving] iniquity, rebellion, and sin."

God is altogether beautiful, sees our ugly wrongs, and still lovingly embraces us, giving us chance after chance to do right.

So no, you are not your failures. Dealing with mistakes and regrets is strenuous, but Christ gives freedom from it all. You'll take gratitude to a new level once you begin to grasp how He loves you and graces you, just because.

Because of Grace

One of the best examples of God loving us because of grace is Peter. Peter, the outspoken disciple. Peter, the disciple who wanted to know who would betray Jesus and then later cut off the ear of the soldier who came to arrest Jesus. Peter, the one who disowned that same Jesus *three* times the same night of the betrayal.

If I were Peter, I'd be a nervous wreck seeing Jesus after the resurrection. A whole hot mess. Jesus wasn't fazed, however. He used that moment to show grace. He didn't disown Peter. Instead, He commissioned him (John 21:15–19).

What does that mean for you?

Any time you fall, get back up, because God has a certain mission for your life. Understand that your purpose doesn't just dissipate after you disappoint God. Thank Christ because you can still come to the throne with an apology on your lips and repentance in your heart. Thank Him because He died for what you're struggling with, way before you even came into existence. Thank Him because He will use the downfalls of your past to elevate your future.

Psalm 103:2–5 encourages us: "Praise the Lord, my soul, and forget not all his benefits—who forgives all your sins and heals all your diseases, who redeems your life from the pit and crowns you with love and compassion, who satisfies your desires with good things so that your youth is renewed like the eagle's" (NIV).

Not only does God forgive you for what you did; He also heals you, redeems you, crowns you, and satisfies you with good things! Our past may be ugly, but that doesn't mean God won't make our future beautiful. What you used to do or what you're currently dealing with does not disqualify you from God's treasures He has reserved for you.

The Lord says, "Forget about what's happened; don't keep going over old history. Be alert, be present. I'm about to do something brand-new. It's bursting out! Don't you see it?" (Isa. 43:18 MSG).

Well, do you?

God's grace is wrapped in His love so thick you can't escape it. You may feel your last mistake was the last straw. You may sulk in solitude. You may run away or stray, indulging yourself in the earth's pleasures instead. But He will still chase you.

Jesus, our Shepherd, has a whole flock to tend to, but He will still leave them, going through anything to get you back—because, yes, even one soul matters. Your soul. He won't rest until you're home. And when you do come, He gathers everyone for the biggest, most glorious celebration in heaven (Luke 15:6–7)! There's a celebration in the kingdom for every lost soul that's found. He has grace reserved for you.

That doesn't mean you should take advantage of it, however. God isn't a foolish ruler who will allow us to use Him. The loving Father also disciplines. Living a life of queendom does not insulate us from the consequences of our actions.

Proverbs 3:11–12 warns us to "not despise the LORD's discipline" and not to "resent his rebuke" (NIV), because only a good Father would discipline His child. It is a demonstration of love.

Perhaps what you're going through isn't a result of your actions at all. Perhaps something happened that was out of your hands. Perhaps you find yourself a victim of a cruel, disheartening past.

I don't know or feel the depths of the hurt and trauma you've experienced. I am not here to categorize your pain, shame, and humiliation into one group. I am not here to minimize it. I earnestly pray you embrace your transformation from victim to victor, through Christ Jesus.

Yes, He can use even *that* thing. Prayer won't change what happened, and, no, we won't forget. But when we release the shackles of shame Satan tries to entangle around us, when we begin to look at our situations through the lens of our forgiving Father, when we begin to see our circumstances as a chance to grow and effectively rule for the kingdom . . . we'll view our struggles and imperfections as training ground.

> Endure hardship as discipline; God is treating you as his children. For what children are not disciplined by their father? If you are not disciplined—and everyone undergoes discipline—

> then you are not legitimate, not true sons and daughters at all. . . . God disciplines us for our good, in order that we may share in his holiness. No discipline seems pleasant at the time, but painful. Later on, however, it produces a harvest of righteousness and peace for those who have been trained by it. (Heb. 12:7–8; 10–11 NIV)

Life is a great teacher; however, we have the Top Educator leading us to glory. He even uses the very situations we run from so that we may teach and be of help to others. Many of us say we want God to use us but are shocked by what is actually required. Sis, experience is what takes our ministries from unreachable to relatable. If we want to help others, God will place us in these uncomfortable positions so *when* we've overcome, we can directly pour into someone else's situation. Whether it be a crowd of thousands, our little sisters, or a mere stranger, the teachings of our past will touch those around us.

Forever Crown

God will guide us as we reign. Unlike with earthly heirs, no amount of falling will disgrace you from the crown God assigned for you. You can't be denounced. You can't say you don't want to rule. Well, actually you can say so, but you'd be talking for nothing! As long as you have accepted Christ, your crown cannot be removed. Your queen status is permanent.

Your crown may be heavy, but it is undoubtedly yours. You may feel the weight of the crown, but God does not pressure you to be perfect. God does not pressure you to the point where you fear you'll lose it. The weight of the world isn't on your shoulders as you rule. It's on His. You may *feel* the weight of it from time to time, or maybe even every day, but understand that God's grace is sufficient for you.

It is in our weakest moments that Christ can show Himself strong (2 Cor. 12:9). No, we cannot be the perfect role model all on our own. It is the power of the Holy Spirit that will give us the strength to keep going. We can't allow our failures and shortcomings to whisper that we aren't fit to reign. The more we read His Word, the more we get to know God for who He really is and change our running from Him into running *to* Him.

The world may not give second chances, but Christ does. Seconds, and thirds, and fourths. His love is never-ending, and His mercies are new every morning (Lam. 3:22–23).

You are not who you were yesterday, last month, or years ago. You have a new life—live like it! When you decided you were going to live for God, He saved every inch of you, transforming you from the inside out. "Anyone who belongs to Christ has become a new person. The old life is gone; a new life has begun!" (2 Cor. 5:17).

While rulers on earth face the constant threat of losing their throne, you can sit still in confidence. You cannot be overthrown, nor can you step down. God's grace protects your crown.

Kingdom Keys

- You can't outrun God—His love chases after you.
- There is nothing that can disqualify us from our crowns or the love of our Father.
- We serve a God of second (times a trillion) chances!

Reflection: *What are things you or someone else has done that you struggle with forgiving? How does God's grace affect that? What are some of the lies Satan attempts to convince you of?*

Here's how to refute Satan's lies: I created a list of queenly biblical affirmations with you in mind! For your gift, head over to adornedinarmor.com/biblical-affirmations.

FAIREST OF THEM ALL

Poison

"Mirror, mirror, on the wall, who's the fairest of them all?"

You know the story.

Every single morning, an evil queen obsessed with her appearance would ask her magical mirror who was the most beautiful in the land. The mirror would always answer that, indeed, the queen was.

Until one day, she wasn't.

The day everything changed, the mirror pointed out to the queen that Snow White is "a thousand times more beautiful than you."[1]

Ouch.

Clearly, the queen wasn't happy with that answer and enlisted a huntsman to murder the young beauty. She thought her problem was resolved . . . until she asked the mirror again.

"Who's the fairest in the land?"

The mirror's answer remained the same: it wasn't her.

The huntsman had deceived the evil queen, and she couldn't rest. Her dissatisfaction grew more and more every day as she became obsessed with murdering Snow White herself. She tried many tactics and failed, but she was relentless. Thinking of the perfect plan, she finally put Snow White in a deep sleep with one bite from her poisonous apple.

As outsiders, we dismiss the queen and write her off as evil, but I found a commonality we share. We too desire full satisfaction with ourselves. Don't you?

When you look into your mirror, does it tell you you're beautiful?

Perhaps some days. Your best days—you know, when your hair lies perfectly and there's not a blemish on your skin. When you've glued on lashes in record-breaking time, chosen the most flattering lipstick that brings out the color of your eyes, and glided your eyeliner with precision that could cut paper.

Or maybe you tried the latest in Korean skincare—a rejuvenating face mask—and it's working wonders for your hard-to-please skin. You look in the mirror and smile to see an elastic, glowing, and smooth surface.

Those days. Your mirror does call you beautiful on those days. But on the others? It can be hurtful.

Your mirror tells you that you're not prettier than *her*. You're not pretty *like* her. You could never be her.

"Her," the gorgeous girl on campus all the guys are crazy about. "Her," the upgraded you—the one who lost ten pounds and bought the new extensions you found on sale. "Her," your favorite celebrity flaunting her latest procedures.

"Her," the one you think is "a thousand times more beautiful" than you.

Like the queen, we've found dissatisfaction with our mirrors. On our end, however, it's been a scam all along.

Yes, girl. Our mirrors have lied.

It's not our own eyes that first deceive us. Our own eyes aren't what make us believe something is wrong with the way we look.

It's the reflection of society. It's social media and pressures from our peers and family and . . . just everything. And we believe them.

Living in the satisfaction of likes and comments to soothe our egos and bruised self-esteem. Masking our hate with false self-love activities. Following the latest trends to try everything, anything to make us prettier. (You know the ones: freezing your face for $400, blood masks, Cheetos facials, and setting appointments with famous Instagram plastic surgeons for fifteen-minute nose jobs.)

Why?

Judgment is the farthest thing from my heart; I just want us to search ours. Ask yourself, sis: Do you try these things out of interest? A little enhancement? Or is it because you adhere to what the world tells you?

Are you believing the lies that say if you don't look like a model or those girls on MTV, you'll never get a man? That if you're not getting enough likes, your appearance isn't likeable?

Your mirror will make you feel there's nothing you can do but try your best at making yourself pretty "like her." Envy leads to evil thoughts toward yourself and your sister, even downplaying her beauty at times.

You love her, but you hate her.

You may not have enlisted a huntsman, but you have enlisted your own hurts. You try to love her, but really you hate you.

The evil queen hated herself. She found beauty in her reflection only when she had it all and behaved irrationally when she lost the very thing that gave her a reason to live. She thought she was healing herself by getting rid of her competition with her last trick. True love's kiss may have given life to Snow White, but the lack of self-love brought death upon the queen.

A part of your heart dies every time you look at another woman and feel *less than*. It dies when you puff yourself up with material things. It dies as a companion to God's grief as He watches you striving—again and again—to be someone He didn't create you to be.

But there is a pulse still beating within you because you have purpose. You've been poisoned, and it's time to come out of that deep sleep, to stop the mindless scrolling on Instagram as you wait for someone—anyone—to tell you you're beautiful.

Are you too far gone? Do you enjoy the taste of the deception that is being fed to you everywhere you look? Or do you want to wake up from this terrible nightmare?

Most of us are too poisoned to see that God calls us poetry. The Passion Translation of Ephesians 2:10 can convince us: "We have become his poetry, a re-created people that will fulfill the destiny he has given each of us, for we are joined to Jesus, the Anointed One."

Writer Jon Bloom says it perfectly: "Your poem contains all the comedic and tragic drama of an existence more real and more meaningful than you have yet to comprehend. If you think you are a boring work of prose, you don't yet see things as they really are. You are afflicted with a sin-induced cataract in the eye of the heart. But it is God's intention and delight to heal your sight."[2]

Nothing about you is uninteresting! Don't you want to rip off the mask and see it for yourself? Don't you want to shatter the mirror and reflect the love of God? Don't you want Him to heal your eyesight?

Say yes. All you have to say is yes.

He heard you.

And now, God is beginning to redirect your mind away from the falsities you've been believing for too long. The dosage was lethal, the lies they told you. It'll take a while for the fog to clear, a while until you can see that God means it.

You don't have to measure yourself by the people plastered on magazines. You are who God wants. Just as you are.

You are His masterpiece. You are an epic. You are art.

As queens, we should all believe this. Everything God creates deserves a place in a gallery. He particularly takes pride in us, the human race. We were made in the glorious, matchless likeness of Him.

He rejoices over you, gazing at you in love. A van Gogh, He would paint the very same brushstrokes to make you just as you are, over and over again. He made no mistake the first time.

And though you willingly took a bite of the apple, hungrily gulping it down, you can be saved. Only in this story, an earthly prince won't be the remedy. There's no more banishment, no more hiding when the Prince of Peace is near.

Jesus can wake you from your slumber and make you fall in love with the very things your mirror has told you to hate.

You'll awaken with the kiss of His loving-kindness toward you. Your reflection will become clear, comparison-free, beautiful. You will fall in love with the poetry that is you, just as God does.

No Filter

Tyra may have taught me how to walk with a book on my head, but my mother taught me to represent myself well at all times. Ever since I was a little girl, I was conditioned to constant grooming. I knew my hair must always be presentable, my face should be powdered, and my clothes should always be ironed.

When my mom and I need new foundation, we go to Sephora together. If I'm pondering a new hairstyle, I scrounge the internet to find her the perfect photo. We send texts asking each other for advice on great deals we find at the mall. Beauty tips came with the package of growing into my womanhood.

If my mother saw me slouching, she'd simply look over at me and I'd know to stand upright. In my rebellion, I'd at times slouch on purpose, and she would playfully press her hand into my back, making it flat. Yeah, envision that!

While my mom taught me all the surface-level basics, the real foundation of our relationship is the heart things. She reminds me of my beauty and worth every single day, showing me how to carry myself with respect and dignity, and encouraging me about the promise of my future.

Her words and actions aren't the only components that illustrate the huge, gracious, and loving heart she has. She is beauty, dignity, and hope personified. I have the utmost respect for her, not just because she's my mom but because God blessed me with her.

And it is because of her that I know exactly what inner beauty looks like.

In raising the young women of our household, my mother taught us to pay close attention to our hearts. I'm not talking about the corny mess of "listening" to it. I'm talking about the spiritual condition.

What's in it? What flows from it? Who does it beat for?

For my mom, it's God. She taught my sisters and me that holy women put their hope in Him. John Piper puts it like this:

> At the core of all godly women, cemented in the soul, there is a simple but steadfast hope in God. . . . These godly women adorn their souls with a peculiar beauty: not base servility or brash power, but a combination of humility and lion-like courage that the world cannot explain. The world cannot make women this way. Their beauty comes from somewhere—from someone—else. With their souls beautified by God, Christian women display Jesus in such a way that unbelievers may be won to Christ, even without a word being spoken.[3]

Pretty powerful, huh? You have that influence when you adorn yourself with the Word of God. The Bible tells us, "Let your true beauty come from your inner personality, not a focus on the external. For lasting beauty comes from a gentle and peaceful spirit, which is precious in God's sight and is much more important than the outward adornment of elaborate hair, jewelry, and fine clothes" (1 Pet. 3:3–4 TPT).

Women of God are not bodies to be gawked at. We weren't created for the male gaze; we were created to celebrate ourselves on the inside and out. So no, God isn't telling you to let yourself go. In fact, the term *cosmetics* derives from the Greek term *kosmos*, which is a harmonious arrangement.[4] Looking good looks great to God. Whether we're attracted to the sky or the latest product at Sephora, we have a desire for beauty, arrangement, and design, and that comes from Him.

But we do have an issue when we are *more* concerned with our outward appearance than our inner appearance. Our hope doesn't lie in our clothes or our looks; it's in Christ. Christlikeness is the core of all God has created us to be. We should rely on God and we should rest in Him, meaning our souls are safe in His plans. We don't "do the most." We do less because God is handling our situation. He brings us peace.

It is that same blessed assurance that makes us bold and fearless. Though my mom can no longer physically walk without pain, she has set her gaze on the path God has called her to walk spiritually. She isn't afraid of her illness. She prays to God about her future and that of her marriage, ministry, and children. My mom confidently secures the kingdom here on earth by unabashedly submitting to God's model for womankind, marriage, maternity, and ministry.

The woman of God has a beautiful heart, but that doesn't mean she won't fall. Writer Amanda Criss says:

> And though she stumbles like Sarah and laughs in disbelief at the promises of her God, He will turn her laughter into one

> of confidence in her Savior and joyful hope in His word. By faith, she laughs, because she looks to that lasting city, the heavenly one. By faith, she joins the ranks of holy women who considered Him faithful who had promised. She is a woman of whom this world is not worthy, and God is not ashamed to be called her God.[5]

I know we're talking about women here, but King David had the best description of beholding God's beauty of all time. The New Living Translation relates his prayer in Psalm 27:4: "The one thing I ask of the Lord—the thing I seek most—is to live in the house of the Lord all the days of my life, delighting in the Lord's perfections and meditating in his Temple."

Imagine being satisfied with merely gazing upon the glorious God as David was! As believers, we will begin to enjoy connecting to God by delighting in His beauty too.

Satan, of course, doesn't want this for us. Russian novelist Fyodor Dostoyevsky once reflected, "Beauty is the battlefield where God and Satan contend with each other for the hearts of men."[6]

How true is that?

The fight is constant. We experience the tugs from the world, warping our minds to abide by their temporary terms of beauty, and on the other hand, God is calling us to gaze upon something much greater, a beauty that will last forever.

In Psalm 27, David chose the latter. In a time of David's own terrifying and personal storms of insecurity, rejection, unpredictability, and fear, Satan tried to put a filter of negativity over David's eyes. He attempted to discourage him by reminding him of his troubles; however, David chose to keep his eyes on the beauty of the Lord.

We too face insecurity, rejection, unpredictability, and fear. We experience things we don't deserve; we are let down, and bitterness tries to force its way into us. The enemy wants us to give in to defeat and darkness, so we live our lives blinded to the makeover we get in Christ. But we are to be like King David!

When we encounter God's beauty, He conceals our dark spots and becomes the foundation in our hearts. It polishes our souls and renews our minds. The more we look to God and not the reflection of our hurts and trials, the more we transform into His likeness.

> We can all draw close to him with the veil removed from our faces. And with no veil we all become like mirrors who brightly reflect the glory of the Lord Jesus. We are being transfigured into his very image as we move from one brighter level of glory to another. And this glorious transfiguration comes from the Lord, who is the Spirit. (2 Cor. 3:18 TPT)

Encountering God's beauty gives you freedom. It empowers you to be fearless, to trust in Him and rest in His promises. It trickles into every aspect of your life and shows you how to find beauty in yourself and even in the people who have wronged you.

Becoming filled with God's beauty is like constantly heading to Sephora to restock on the essentials in your makeup bag. You can't afford to ever leave it out of your routine. Emulating God's beauty is an inside job—one He performs with no filter.

Bloom

My mother showed my sisters and me that real beauty comes from knowing who we saw when we looked in the mirror. Daughters of the King of Kings. Royalty.

And it is important we carry ourselves as such.

Contrary to society's standards, having a done-up face and the most tasteful clothing isn't the most important thing in life. Having a heart led by the Spirit of God is. Real beauty comes from the ability to bear fruit.

In Galatians 5:22–23, the Bible says the Holy Spirit produces the fruit of love, joy, peace, patience, kindness, goodness, faithfulness, gentleness, and self-control.

Don't panic! It is only when we accept God into our lives that we can bear the fruit of the Spirit. It's not by our own might. The Holy Spirit is the One who empowers us to grow.

A little more background: The Holy Spirit is a person. I know, it may sound weird. But get this, the Bible illustrates that God is three persons in one! There is only one God, of course. However, He is manifested, or appears, as God the Father, God the Son, and God the Holy Spirit—the Holy Trinity. These persons are equal.

It's hard to explain—even the great Billy Graham chose not to do so. We accept the Trinity by faith.

The Holy Spirit makes our hearts beautiful. The Spirit convicts you (John 16:8). He also produces the fruit of the Spirit.

We have a powerful person *freely* producing fruit within us. It's not based on our striving and efforts. These virtues of the Spirit are produced after the rain and toils of life. You'll feel growing pains in the pruning process, as God strips you of the very things that do you no good. You'll find your shiny fruit after the sunshine and soil provide the proper nutrients.

It'll be rough because you'll still find old parts of you there, dormant, waiting to sprout up in the midst of your fruit. Your former self will attempt to take control again. However, we have the decision to choose either the old us or the new life the Spirit gives.

We have all the help we need. Jesus is the vine, God is the gardener, and the Holy Spirit produces the fruit. Jesus explains the analogy in John 15. God, the gardener,

> cuts off every branch of mine that doesn't produce fruit, and he prunes the branches that do bear fruit so they will produce even more. You have already been pruned and purified by the message I have given you. Remain in me, and I will remain in you. For a branch cannot produce fruit if it is severed from the vine, and you cannot be fruitful unless you remain in me. (vv. 2–4)

Did you breathe a sigh of relief yet?

Great. You can let go of the pressure to be "good"—we can't achieve any of these virtues on our own.

We've been getting the idea wrong the whole time. True beauty may be found within you, but it doesn't begin in you. It is first found through Christ. And it can only grow when we keep close to Him. The fruit of the Spirit are produced when we walk by faith.

Walking by faith may mean believing in your beauty because God said so. It's trusting God will come through with those issues you're insecure about. It's praying and not worrying over those obstacles that seem like they won't budge.

Walking by faith is living totally dependent on what the Word says and not what the world says. Therefore, we must be rooted in Christ.

When we rely on Him for our daily dose of nutrients, we bloom. If you have concerns about the unattractive and dead parts within you, allow Him to sever those parts too. If you have weeds entangling your heart, God will relieve you from their suffocation.

Stay close to Him and you will see: you will overflow with love and joy. You will radiate with joy and peace. You won't struggle so much with patience and kindness. Your life will radiate goodness and faithfulness. You will emulate gentleness and self-control.

It won't be easy, but we won't get there with our own works. We are God's workmanship, and it is through Christ that we are chiseled to perfection. If we allow ourselves to be pliant as clay in our Potter's hands, we will bear fruit and will be able to perceive a beauty that radiates from the inside out.

Is the Holy Spirit living in your heart? Living life centered on God is the only way we'll see beauty in our own gardens. It is the only way His beauty will be reflected in us.

Kingdom Keys

- God sees you as a work of art because He formed you with His very hands.
- When we are envious of other women, we lose our identity trying to measure ourselves to their standards.

- God sees the depth of who we are and wants us to come before Him without a veil. He wants all of us, even our flaws.
- The Holy Spirit comforts, reassures, and plants the truth of God inside our hearts.
- Beauty fades, but the kingdom of God stands forever. Think of these things, not of the temporary fixes on earth.
- We look to God for beauty and find freedom in a Lord who makes no mistakes.

Reflection: *What does your mirror tell you? Are you ready to change how you perceive yourself?*

Girl, mark your mirror! It's time for the #ClaimYourCrown Challenge. Grab your Kylie Lip Kit or your Fenty Beauty gloss (a marker and sticky note works too—I'm just extra). As a declaration and reminder to yourself, write, "Society's mirror is poison, but God calls me poetry." Don't forget to hashtag #ClaimYourCrown to be connected to a whole community of sisters and so I can repost!

Six

THE ROYAL TREATMENT

From a young age, we're quickly taught life isn't fair. At recess, you held your breath in hopes you wouldn't be the last one chosen to join a kickball team. In junior high, you realized that as stereotypical as it sounds, the cool kids do run the school. And then you grew up to discover you can't buy that gown for formal because you aren't rich enough. You can't attend that college because you're not smart enough. You can't have the promotion because you're not "man" enough.

It seems as if life is a series of blinking red "access denied" signs. We are watching from the outside of glass doors and below glass ceilings. We face situations where we are left out but have a front row seat to the woman who seems to have it all.

VIP status, however, isn't only for the boss woman in the office with a view. VIP status is also for the assistant, the receptionist, the janitor, and the man on the street you hope to skip by. VIP status even applies to the very people you don't like.

It isn't solely for the popular. It isn't only for the rich. It isn't only for those society says it's reserved for. VIP status is for you.

You can forget the status quo—we take orders from the ultimate Commander in Chief. Those you feel have the constant upper hand aren't better. You don't have to be in someone's entourage to have the hookup. Because you are a part of God's family, He escorts you in.

Dismiss the notion that special treatment is solely for celebrities, leading public figures, or your local "It Girl." As children of God, we are precious and we too have favor.

Noah had it. At a time when wickedness was especially rampant, God remembered Noah as the only one who never lost sight of Him. When Noah tried to warn everyone else about impending doom, they mocked, scoffed, and laughed. In the end, God protected Noah and his family from the floodgates of judgment and destruction.

David had it. The shepherd boy went from being overlooked by his own family to being personally requested by Prophet Samuel and later crowned king.

Joseph had it. He lived in a dysfunctional home with brothers so jealous of their father's adoration for him that they sold him into slavery. God demonstrated His unending favor by never leaving him, equipping him with wisdom to find goodwill with Egypt's pharaoh, and later elevating him to become a ruler himself. The very brothers who sold him came crawling back for help when a famine hit.

But what exactly is this "favor"?

I love Pastor Steven Furtick's definition for it: "God's favor is the guarantee of His presence and the provision of His power to accomplish His special purpose in and through your life. It's intended not for your convenience, but for His purpose, and it doesn't mean your life is going to get any easier. In fact, it almost certainly guarantees that your life is going to get harder."[1]

Noah, David, and Joseph were not exempt. We briefly hit on a few Bible stories that depict God's favor and the struggles that ensued. However, we can't go on with the topic of God's favor without talking about one of the stories that probably best depicts it.

The book of Esther.

Here's how it goes down: God uses a beautiful Jewish girl to save her nation after she finds favor with the king. The end.

I find that most of us, including myself, tend to see the story of Esther as one that has little struggle. Because the story is "pretty," we fail to see just how powerful it really is. We see her purpose closely tied to her appearance. However, when we dig deeper, we find there's a bigger message behind saving her people.

First, Esther was an orphan. She was taken in by her older cousin, Mordecai, and was raised as his daughter. Perhaps you knew this already, but I wanted to start off with that point because I've read and heard the story of Esther numerous times and never once thought about how she must've felt. Maybe you haven't either?

Maybe you didn't think about how heartbroken she must've been, living without a mother to guide her and a father to dote on her. Maybe you didn't think about the strenuous life she lived as a descendant of an oppressed ethnic group.

Not only did she lose her parents; she also lost her home when she was whisked away to a new place to be groomed for a man she didn't know. When she was chosen as queen in one of the earliest beauty pageants, her life didn't get easier from there.

Or maybe you did consider these things but didn't give them much thought.

Either way, I feel you.

The Bible mentions Esther was an orphan Jew and goes right along with the story. We don't have time to even register her background. When you read any other book, you tend to know how the protagonist is feeling. You know what they are thinking. In this short story, you don't.

Church culture repeatedly tells us we must apply the Word of God in our lives, but often we don't think to position ourselves in the places of the people whose lives we read about. We look for the moral of the story and take all the other details at face value. However, when we begin to study the people and recognize their humanity, we can see just how involved, methodic, and all-powerful God was in their lives.

Funny thing is, the book of Esther is the only Bible book that doesn't mention God. The author was very strategic in writing Esther's story. By leaving God out, the author encourages us to look for Him throughout. The International Bible Society couldn't have said it better:

> It appears that the author has deliberately refrained from mentioning God or any religious activity as a literary device to heighten the fact that it is God who controls and directs all the seemingly insignificant coincidences that make up the plot and issue in deliverance for the Jews. God's sovereign rule is assumed at every point, an assumption made all the more

> effective by the total absence of reference to him. It becomes clear to the careful reader that Israel's Great King exercises his providential and sovereign control over all the vicissitudes of his beleaguered covenant people.[2]

Okay, okay. I'll stop right there and spare you the rhetoric and composition lessons. But I definitely learned some things.

Esther's story isn't *just* the narrative of pauper to princess. God used Esther to shatter glass ceilings *in* cultures. Teaming up with Mordecai, she became a leader in a male-dominated society and rescued the Jewish people from being exterminated. Together, they took the Jewish people from peril to praise.

You see, in reading the Bible, we don't have to be on the outside looking in. We have access to the Author of life because of Christ. God left us this guide to help us draw near to Him—to remember we belong. We have access to so much more than words on a page. We will miss the small ways God mightily comes through if we don't meditate on all presented before us.

The Bible invites us to ask questions. It challenges us to experience it. The Bible reminds us we are favored right where we are.

The story of Queen Esther is a redemptive piece reminding us that God's people are never really overlooked. God sees us. He not only empathizes with our pain but also feels it. Our maltreatment never goes unnoticed. He's taking note and is preparing to act.

God had a plan and favored Esther while she was back at home with her people; He had a plan and favored her in the palace. Where you are and where you come from have nothing to do with God's love for you. He has made us all distinctly beautiful and will use us for His glory no matter our background.

I didn't always entirely connect with mine. My background, I mean. As a Haitian growing up in America, I found it difficult to celebrate my country when I never experienced it for myself. All around me, my friends and family had Haitian pride that I'd primarily see at home, family events, or church. My family would always speak so highly of their experiences back home.

In an excerpt of my life experience from an article I wrote for *Teen Vogue*, I shared:

> I understood Creole but didn't speak it. I loved music but had no interest in the Kompa genre. I savored the phenomenal flavors of Haitian foods . . . but I never attempted to cook it.
>
> My elementary, middle and high school were located in an exceptionally diverse suburb. There were the cliques of popular kids and then there were the groups everyone shunned: the outcasts. It was an unspoken yet universally-acknowledged rule that the outcasts were not to be associated with. They were the Haitians, Mexicans, and Africans; they were the undesirables. It wasn't uncommon to hear taunts like "Eww, you're Mexican" or "African Booty Scratcher" hurled down the hallway as these kids—mostly new immigrants—fought through the huddles of students crowding around their lockers.
>
> Being called a Haitian was the biggest insult. Synonymous with ugly, dirty, and ashy, the Haitian ethnicity was tossed around as an expletive. It was a verbal dagger that a bully might pull out of their back pocket to get the biggest "oohs" in the room. For most of my peers, Haiti was reserved for one

> paragraph in their history textbook. It was this foreign land that was unbearably hot and desolate, with poverty ravaging the streets.[3]

I knew this wasn't true. Though many of those who thought this way considered themselves "friends" of mine, I never understood why there was so much hate around Haiti.

Then I grew up. I learned about how much of a treasure it was and why the island was so oppressed. I learned about the legacy of slavery there and the world's refusal to recognize this. I learned about the greed and the indifference capitalism brings. I learned how the world often forgets all people are worth fighting for.

It wasn't until I experienced Haiti for myself that I learned how to efficiently fight for my country. I was able to fully embrace all of me when I went "home." This has led me to write for and be featured by the *Haitian Times* and *Teen Vogue* and to honor my island through my pageant platforms.

Want to know the funny part? My trip occurred a mere few weeks after President Trump made disparaging comments about Haiti and African countries at an Oval Office meeting.

While I was in Haiti, I was adamant in showcasing its beauty through a piece for *Teen Vogue* and my vlog. Those who came across the content were honestly baffled—they never considered Haiti to be anything but desolate, let alone a vacation spot. They didn't know any good could come from Haiti.

But God is using this Haitian girl. While higher officials may dismiss my culture, I can stand unashamed because God made me on purpose—for His purpose. He has blessed me. He has used my culture and my country—a place people considered undesirable—to highlight how His favor can make an impact regardless of where you come from.

When you come to understand whose you are, you begin to see the favor you have over your life. Whether your peers aren't making room for you on the team or your voice is being quieted in the boardroom—rely on God to make that space for you. He's already done so in heaven; surely, He will on earth. Whether your life is a playground, a battlefield, or a palace, God will always choose you first.

He will also protect you as the prize you are. He will cater to your needs as if you were the only person on His mind. The Bible is constantly telling us God is going to take care of us. My favorite passage involves a bird analogy: "Look at the birds. They don't plant or harvest or store food in barns, for your heavenly Father feeds them. And aren't you far more valuable to him than they are?" (Matt. 6:26).

God's Word doesn't just end there. He goes on in Luke 12:7, 22–34 to really drill into our heads that we are worth way more than birds, so we have no reason to fear. We're so precious to Him that He knows each and every strand of our hair.

Try to picture that.

Go back to a time when your bangs fell in front of your face and you tried to count the strands, one by one. Or think back to the time you went to the salon for a haircut and your hairdresser got way too scissor-happy and you didn't know the damage until you saw a pile of tufts scattered on the floor.

That's *a lot* of hair.

And God has counted every single follicle, never overlooking one. He pays attention to us on such an intricate level that we can't even begin to fathom how much He finds us valuable.

Kingdom Keys

- God goes before you and makes room for you.
- Esther's story isn't just about the advantages of beauty. It's a reminder that God's people are never overlooked. He sees us. He not only empathizes with us in our pain but also feels it. The way we are being treated never goes unnoticed. He's taking note and is preparing to act.
- There is a reason why God designed, shaped, and placed you. From the color of your skin to the texture of your hair. God has made us all distinctly beautiful and will use us for His glory no matter our background.
- When we read the Bible, we don't have to be on the outside looking in. We have access to the Author of life because of Christ. The Bible is our guide to help us draw near to Him—to remember we belong. We have access to so much more than words on a page. We will miss the small ways God mightily comes through if we don't meditate on what's presented before us.
- The Bible invites you to ask questions. It challenges you to experience it. The Bible reminds you that you are favored right where you are.

Reflection: *Think back to a time when you felt ostracized or looked down upon—maybe it was years ago or maybe it was yesterday. What would you tell yourself in light of what you've just read?*

Seven

THE ROYAL BRIGADE

With divine favor comes divine protection. God promises you security.

Have you ever thought about the intricacy of the royal family security procedures at Kensington or Buckingham Palace, or just how much it may all cost?

Their protection costs are not public information (I checked!) but are undoubtedly high. From protection at the home base to traveling with their security and entourage, it's likely to be millions of dollars a year. The royals have an additional police force, the Fixated Threat Assessment Centre, utilized to prevent attacks. It was created in 2006, partially due to rising dangers such as an almost successful carjacking and close calls in the palace.[1]

How about security protocol for the closest thing the US has to our own royal palace—the White House? The White

House stays secure in many ways, but we have a little insight into a few of them.

- Want to tour the White House? You can, in part—just as long as you submit your application at least twenty-one days prior. This gives security enough time to perform background checks and keep a steady head count. (When I studied in Washington for a semester, I discovered they were backed up for months!)
- Bulletproof windows. An attacker once shot seven rounds and not one made a crack in the glass. Talk about impenetrable.
- No drones allowed, with the exception of those of the Secret Service, of course.
- Absolutely no planes overhead. The White House has missiles, but the public has no idea where they are.
- A monstrous fence that is eleven feet of steel and rebar. It has spikes so no one can climb over, it stops vehicles, and it also alerts security once there's pressure on it.
- Infrared lasers everywhere. These lasers sense even the slightest threat while blanketing the sky, surface, and underground.[2]

What I found most interesting is the anatomy of the Presidential Motorcade. It's essentially the White House on wheels with everything you can imagine.[3] Think medical facilities, press corps, a communications station, a personal contingency response force, and, of course, internet and phone connection.

There are about sixteen to twenty presidential limousines, and a motorcade is sent ahead to the president's every destination prior to his arrival. While he is on his way, two helicopters hover close by in case of emergency.

The Presidential Motorcade is composed of a vast array of vehicles with a specific schedule. The precise arrangement is altered based on the expedition and assets available; however, there is a central layout. The car the president occupies, aka "Stagecoach," is the main focus, as all activities are focused on ensuring the car gets to its destination.

There's always at least one "dupe" (called "Spare") accompanying Stagecoach in case of car problems or attacks. It's the perfect decoy. The vehicles have identical license plates and intertwine in and out to further conceal the president and confuse attackers. The Secret Service also throws in extra vehicles from time to time. But just because these are all on the move doesn't necessarily mean the president is inside one of them.

Overall, when the president is on a journey, his limousine is at the middle of the motorcade. What we've come to know as "The Beast" (thanks, prime-time television) is a luxurious, indomitable vehicle packed with unimaginable capabilities suited to protect the president during all forms of attack. These capabilities include night-vision systems, state-of-the-art ballistic armoring, a secured compartment with an air supply (yeah, I have no idea how they did that either), and even a supply of the president's blood type.

Because presidents and royal families are dominant, influential figures, it's necessary to protect them at all costs.

Isn't it crazy that our Father thinks the same of us? The lengths mere men go through for protection is almost incomprehensible, but the surveillance of our heavenly Father supersedes all that.

We have state-of-the-art, round-the-clock security and don't have to pay for it. We don't even need to have worldly status to obtain it.

There are unseen battles that God has conquered on our behalf and we don't even think about it. He has delivered us from the snare of the enemy. He is protecting us, and to demonstrate how special we are to Him, He has commanded angels to keep watch. Psalm 91:11 tells us we have angels concerned about us and guarding us wherever we go.

When Elijah escaped to the wilderness, praying for death to come, God sent an angel to encourage him to eat (1 Kings 19:5). When you too feel you can't go on, God will provide you the strength you need to live.

When Daniel was wrongfully thrown into jail, God sent His angel to shut the mouths of the lions, leaving Daniel unscathed (Dan. 6:20–23). When you too are wrongfully accused, pray that God clamps the mouth shut of the very thing out to destroy you.

We can expect all of this because when we fear God, we are raised up with Christ and seated in heavenly places (Eph. 2:6).

The Secret Service can't compare. God and His angels are the real masters of security. He already has taken note of your enemies' weaknesses and strengths and has equipped His highly trained angel armies to fight on your behalf. They don't need scenarios to learn what they must do. The invincible God always protects, always perseveres.

Before getting back into this book, you were probably exposed to senseless killings while scrolling through Instagram, your favorite television show may have been interrupted with breaking news of a catastrophe somewhere in the world, or you probably had to silence the violence in your own home.

You're probably wondering, *If I'm so well protected, why does God allow horrible things to happen to me? Why are there tragedies around the world?*

I can honestly say I don't have the answer. But the more I grow in my faith, the more I learn that none of us can escape evil because the world itself is just that—evil.

God wants us to rely on Him even when we are at the end of ourselves. We often champion Job for his experience of losing it all, but it wasn't easy. There were tears, the feeling of rejection, and ostracization—even his wife goaded him to curse God.

However, Job kept in mind that God was all He needed. I too have experienced how even in devastation, God protects me. The pain and destruction won't last. Heaven awaits us.

So while I may not have the direct answer, I have a direct line.

Kingdom Keys

- The Secret Service can't compare. God and His angels are the real masters of security. He has already taken note of your enemies' weaknesses and strengths and has equipped His highly trained angel armies to fight on your behalf. They don't need scenarios to learn what they must do. The invincible God always protects, always perseveres.

- Pain and destruction won't always be our portion.

Reflection: *What moment in your life caused you to doubt God's protection? Do you struggle with this now? Are there signs of your pain transforming into purpose?*

Eight

WISHES DON'T ALWAYS COME TRUE

God is not a genie.

Upon hearing that quote, I murmured "mmm" like a child savoring something sweet for the first time. I loved the brevity of the statement and envisioned that blue larger-than-life genie—you know, from *Aladdin*—being held against his will in the magic lamp. Then I attempted to see God in His place, held captive by the wishes and weight of our expectations. And of course, I couldn't. The picture dared not form.

God does not whirl into our lives after we rub some inanimate object; He doesn't show up when our eyes are squeezed shut, head tilted toward the stars. He is a constant presence and is shackle-free. I revel in knowing we have absolutely no power over Him and that He constantly sees us.

Instagram was the first place I saw it. The quote, I mean. Again and again. And then I *heard* it again and again. By preachers eager to relate to millennials, by influencers who needed a quote to match their Instagram aesthetic.

And then the words lost their magic. The more I saw it, the more I heard it, the more it began to embody watered-down social-media Scripture. It served as a quick explanation for why you don't—why you can't—get what you want. And I realized it insinuates something false.

God isn't a genie, no. But He *does* want to grant us the desires of our hearts (Ps. 37:4). He *does* want to bless His children. If our wants align with His will, it's more likely they will happen, but it's always in God's time and in His way.

Pursue God for His "presence," not His "presents." Seek God for who He is, not for what He can do for you. When you're in constant communication with Him, you'll experience relationship that soothes your soul. You'll experience walking in His will. You'll see how wishes don't always come true, but prayers often do.

Have you ever wanted something so bad? You hoped for it and maybe even dreamed about it, only to not receive it?

Since we were kids, we've been told we won't get everything we want and "money doesn't grow on trees," but that doesn't change that you're left feeling crushed, discouraged, and even angry at God. You subconsciously check off yet another way God didn't come through for you.

Sometimes we go into prayer with a predetermined answer. We have our own agenda, knowing that when we say "amen," we already know what answer we will stick to. God told us no. He sent it through a friend or an email. But because we went into prayer with the "go ahead," we exit with "go ahead."

If you're like me, your problem is that you know God can do "exceedingly abundantly above" all that you could ever ask for or think (Eph. 3:20), but you find yourself questioning if He would really do so for *you*.

I recall so many moments when I felt assured but still uncertain, if that makes sense. I trusted that God has plans for a future and a hope for me (Jer. 29:11), but often I found myself backing away from high expectations. In my mind, it made sense since I had no idea where or when I would be living in that future and hope He promised me.

We live in a society that breeds self-sufficiency. Being about your business is commendable, and God applauds that too. But what He doesn't like is when we rely on our own abilities before Him (Prov. 3:5).

I leave the things I really want and know I can't get on my own in "God's hands." But am I really leaving them in His hands if I'm not praying and fasting about them—if I don't give Him every single thing?

For a long time, I found myself not asking God for the things that were the most important to me: my mom's healing, my desired career position, restoring relationships, and other things about my life. You may be thinking I didn't trust God to come through in those aspects, and while that was partially true, that's not all there is to the story. Subconsciously, I didn't pray for those things because He already knew and knows what I need. I've had many occasions when I simply didn't know what to say . . . and that's okay.

A verse about God that always amazes me is Romans 8:26. I've mentioned it before—God's love is so immense, so palpable, so attentive that He uses the Holy Spirit placed in us to express the feelings we couldn't even explain if we tried. Our groans and heartaches are His language.

I used that as a reason to not bring my requests to God. But man, I was so wrong for that. Yes, reliance on the Holy Spirit is pivotal, but we must take responsibility for the people and problems God has given us to pray over.

After I regained my voice and started speaking to Him again, another "reasoning" showed its face: the belief that "if it's in God's will for our lives, it will happen."

There are a few important factors that come into play here. One being our free will. God may want something for us, but often it may not come to pass because, ultimately, we choose how we want to live. God won't force us to act.

It is when we are in communication with God that we begin to see what His will is. Therefore, when we use the excuse "If it is meant to be, it'll be" to avoid sharing our hearts, it may cause us to become complacent in our prayer lives.

In John 16:24, we see that the one thing keeping us from complete joy is opening our own mouths to make our requests.

Bring your requests to God because it illustrates you believe in Him and His promises. In order to receive, we must have faith. Jesus said, "I tell you the truth, if you had faith even as small as a mustard seed, you could say to this mountain, 'Move from here to there,' and it would move. Nothing would be impossible" (Matt. 17:20).

You probably have experienced some form of betrayal in your life, causing you to lose faith in others. Life's pain burdens us with trust issues. God always gets the brunt of it, even though He has been the only thing in our lives that has been consistent and true.

God doesn't have to prove Himself to us; He's almighty. He supersedes all things and yet will show He has no secret motive. Nothing He grants us comes with a price we can't see coming.

What we need to do is ask God to help our unbelief (Mark 9:24). And on our end, we must attentively wait for God to speak, because contrary to common belief, He does.

Sometimes He speaks through people, sometimes He speaks through dreams, sometimes He speaks through songs. But He will always speak through His Word.

We can't know what God has promised us if we don't even know what He said. In order to hear His voice, we have to know His voice. That begins by immersing ourselves in the Bible, His living, breathing Word.

There is power in persistent prayer (Mic. 7:7). It's more than asking God for things. It's about the relationship. God wants to have a place to meet you every day. More than once. More than the hurried prayer you mumble as you slide your heels on for work and run out the door. He wants you to be desperate to hear from Him.

If you need to journal, if you need to stick Post-it notes all over your mirror and walls, if you need to use a prayer jar, if you need to set an alarm . . . do it. Do whatever it takes to come before the Lord. He's waiting for you.

May we desperately seek God as Hannah did. The Bible depicts her as worn down from her inability to bring forth a child for the man she loved. She faced constant verbal lashing from her rival, her husband's second wife. Though her husband loved Hannah most, she was deeply anguished. One day, her rival provoked her relentlessly to the point where

Hannah couldn't eat. She left home to pray in the house of the Lord. Even in the midst of her bitter tears, she prayed and she prayed and she prayed. She also made a vow: "Lord Almighty, if you will only look on your servant's misery and remember me, and not forget your servant but give her a son, then I will give him to the Lord for all the days of his life, and no razor will ever be used on his head" (1 Sam. 1:11 NIV).

Hannah prayed so fervently that the prophet Eli thought she was drunk. She prayed in her heart—her lips moving, her voice unheard. When Eli told her to put away her wine, she explained she wasn't intoxicated and how burdened she felt by her barrenness. She explained she was "pouring out [her] soul to the Lord" (v. 15 NIV).

After hearing this, Eli assured her to leave in peace, for God would grant her what she desired. Hannah left, holding on to his words. No longer distressed, she was able to eat again.

The next day, Hannah woke up early to worship and then went back home. She and her husband made love, and the Bible says, "The Lord remembered her" (v. 19 NIV). Hannah became pregnant and gave birth to a baby boy. Her son was named Samuel, which means "God has heard."

Hannah was persistent in asking God for her son, becoming a beautiful emblem of what it means to pray ceaselessly. She has shown us we can pray boldly, without restraint. God doesn't want to hear pointless rambling; He wants to hear your heart.

We can wish upon a star all we want, or we can pray to the star-breather, the One who created them. Wishes go unanswered, but our prayers will always be heard by God.

Kingdom Keys

- God is not a genie.
- Pray ceaselessly, not to receive but for relationship.
- Don't be afraid to go to God with your requests. There's no hidden price to pay with praying.

Reflection: *Are there any prayers you're waiting for God to answer? I encourage you to write them down. Ask Him if each one aligns with His will, and pray to accept whatever His final answer may be.*

Nine

BOW DOWN

Rihanna broke the internet. The digital world was in a frenzy after paparazzi captured her in New York City donning a gigantic, red fur coat in the shape of a heart. She was basically a walking Valentine's Day card—the world clamored over her and the coat's design.

It wasn't the coat's first appearance. In 2016, Hedi Slimane, former creative director of Saint Laurent, presented the second portion of his last collection during Paris Fashion Week. He held an exclusive fashion show signifying his "love letter" to Paris, and the final look featured *the* coat retailed at $15,000. There wasn't much buzz about it since the runway show had a strict no-phones policy, but things changed with its first official feature on the summer cover of *W Magazine*, starring "heart-stopper" Cara Delevingne.[1]

After Rihanna made it popular, top fashion figures took to Instagram to share their love for the coveted coat too. Think

Eva Chen featuring her baby bump and Kendall Jenner displaying a "laid back" feel.

Little do they know, these fashion icons are face-to-face in a "who wore it better" battle. The Bible did it first.

The book of Genesis covers the story of a colorful coat that further unleashed covetous behavior among brothers. Joseph, the favored son of Jacob, was gifted from his father the ornate robe that brought heartbreak upon the family.

It wasn't really about the coat, however. It was about favoritism.

Jacob might as well have given Joseph a heart-shaped coat. Though he had twelve sons, he pointedly preferred Joseph the most because he was born in Jacob's old age. Joseph's brothers hated him as much as Jacob loved him and couldn't speak one kind word to him (Gen. 37:4).

The coat ostentatiously displayed how Joseph was favored. That Joseph was "better" than them. And Joseph didn't help his own case when he unwittingly paraded that coat around his brothers and told them he had not one but two dreams about them bowing down to him one day.

In Genesis 37:8, they responded, "'So you think you will be our king, do you? Do you actually think you will reign over us?' And they hated him more because of his dreams and the way he talked about them."

Can you blame them? I mean, *hate* is a pretty strong word, but can you understand why they felt so indignant? Here comes their teenage brother, full of himself because of his father's favor and now seemingly puffing himself up even more so because of his dreams from God. I'd like to think Joseph was just a little naive and wasn't purposely shoving his position in their faces.

However, Joseph's brothers weren't having it; they were overcome with jealousy and pride. They plotted against him, selling him into slavery. To cover their mess, they kept his coat, dipped it in goat's blood, and brought it to their father, hoping he would believe Joseph had been killed by an animal. Jacob mourned for years, heartbroken over his favorite being forever gone.

Even though the story ends with Joseph's dream coming true and the family reuniting, it angers me to know how much Joseph suffered just for being who he was. However, if we take a deeper look into Joseph's life, we can learn a few lessons in humility.

Do you have a walking reminder in your life? Maybe it's a woman who acts like she's better than you? Or it could be the girl who hasn't a care in the world and flaunts her freedom as you struggle.

Or maybe it's you. It's possible you look down on others because you believe you're a better person. You may look at them sideways because they sin differently than you. You judge in your head and give yourself a positive verdict.

Many hatefully judge Christians because they think we act as if we're better. If that's the attitude we're giving off, we're representing Christ poorly.

When we accept God, we become His very own—yes. We are to live out our lives as His chosen people and to lead by example—yes. But we are far from perfect. We can't parade around as if we're sin-free. We all fall short of the glory of God.

As we bear the cross of Christ, it is incredibly important to be cautious of conceit and unhealthy entitlement. Sin is sin: the only reason we are redeemed is because of God's grace. And His grace is available for *everyone*.

A common trait plaguing our world is pridefulness. In fact, in *Mere Christianity,* C. S. Lewis considered it to be the greatest sin. He deemed it to be the vice that no human being can escape: it's one that everyone in the world loathes when they see it in someone else; however, we cannot see it in ourselves.

Lewis also argued that this particular vice is in a league of its own because it was pride that led to Lucifer's downfall. It was through pride that he became the devil. And it is through pride that every other vice is carried out. Pride is the sin that brings dissension.[2]

Proverbs 8:13 reads, "If you respect the Lord, you will hate evil. I hate pride and conceit and deceitful lies" (CEV).

Boom. Wherever there is pride, God isn't in it.

I think it's pretty natural to want to be the best at something. However, we often get ourselves in trouble because our best isn't enough for us, but being *the* best is.

Have you ever struggled when you came across your "equal"? Perhaps you were no longer the smartest student in class because of the new transfer who happened to be a genius. Perhaps you were accustomed to being the most desirable woman in the room until the guy you wanted took an interest in someone else.

Or maybe you're one who cannot bear apologizing to anyone, even if you're wrong. Maybe someone has wronged you, and you're too angry to let them know.

Regardless of the scenario, when we're prideful, we feel displaced, and we're ready to act by any means necessary.

When we have pride, God *will* humble us. In James 4:6, we see, "God opposes the proud but gives grace to the humble."

The two greatest examples of this in the Bible are when God humbled King Nebuchadnezzar and King Herod.

King Nebuchadnezzar got way too cocky, and God had to knock him down a few notches. Or a lot.

> But when his heart and mind were puffed up with arrogance, he was brought down from his royal throne and stripped of his glory. He was driven from human society. He was given the mind of a wild animal, and he lived among the wild donkeys. He ate grass like a cow, and he was drenched with the dew of heaven, until he learned that the Most High God rules over the kingdoms of the world and appoints anyone he desires to rule over them. (Dan. 5:20–21)

Nebuchadnezzar went from living like a royal to living like an animal *until* he realized his position came from God, not himself. He had to suffer severe consequences until he acknowledged God was the true King over all.

Clearly, God does not play. And we see this even more so with King Herod, who was persecuting God's people and had even killed one of Jesus's disciples, James.

> When the day arrived, Herod put on his royal robes, sat on his throne, and made a speech to them. The people gave him a great ovation, shouting, "It's the voice of a god, not of a man!"
>
> Instantly, an angel of the Lord struck Herod with a sickness, because he accepted the people's worship instead of giving

> the glory to God. So he was consumed with worms and died. (Acts 12:21–23)

Sit down, sis! The Word says if we exalt ourselves, we will be humbled. And if we humble ourselves, we will be exalted (Luke 14:11).

Pride hardens our hearts and makes us liars even to ourselves. It allows us to believe we are entitled and deserving of such praise only God deserves. King Nebuchadnezzar was restored to glory; King Herod didn't pass his test.

When you're full of pride, you're full of yourself. And when you're full of yourself, there's no room for God. You can't look up, but you can see straight ahead: your reflection.

God has called His people to live in peace and unity, so all this drama with pride—or drama in general—He opposes. Instead of acting from the standpoint of conceit, we are to consider others as more significant than ourselves. We are to look after their needs more than ours (Phil. 2:3–4).

I know what you might be thinking. This humility thing is hard to accept while living in a me, me, me generation. If we put the needs of others above our own, how can we truly say we love ourselves? I had the same questions.

God isn't saying, "Be a mat," "Roll over," or "Your needs don't matter" (Phil. 2:4). He's saying you achieve greatness when you tend to both, particularly putting other people's interests above your own. And while you take care of others, He will take care of you.

Theologian R. C. Sproul says humility "is not a negative estimation of our own self-worth or a refusal to be honest about our own abilities. . . . We are not . . . to see other people as inherently better than we are because of their talents or position;

rather, we are to count others as more significant than ourselves insofar as we consider their needs before our own."[3]

Paul properly wraps it up: "God has given me grace to speak a warning about pride. I would ask each of you to be emptied of self-promotion and not create a false image of your importance. Instead, honestly assess your worth by using your God-given faith as the standard of measurement, and then you will see your true value with an appropriate self-esteem" (Rom. 12:3 TPT).

When we come to truly experience God's love, we see how much He sees us as His namesakes, and He will do whatever it takes to honor His name. In showing our humility, we boast in the name of Christ.

A Fierce Confidence

Humility is a jam-packed word, but it begins with knowing that God comes first (1 Pet. 5:6). It's knowing that the world will hate us because it first hated our Savior (1 Pet. 2:21–23). It rejoices in truth without shoving it down an adversary's throat (2 Cor. 4:5). Humility is reliant on grace (James 1:21), heeds correction (Prov. 12:15), and also persuades others through love (2 Cor. 5:11).

I *know* how hard it is to adopt humility fully. It doesn't mean we have to be a quiet Goody Two-shoes who runs from adversity. No, with humility, we are even stronger than ever. With it, we are empowered with a Christlike confidence.

As believers, we are to have a gentle and quiet spirit so that we are more in tune to hearing from God (1 Pet. 3:3–4). Having this trait doesn't take away our fierceness. So no, we aren't passive either. We speak up for our cause! There will be times when we won't even have a moment to question our own selves because we will be moved to obey what God wants to fulfill through us.

God is expecting zealousness from His royals. Jesus tells us, "The realm of heaven's kingdom is bursting forth, and passionate people have taken hold of its power" (Matt. 11:12 TPT). If we are both zealous and humble, sin will have no place to rule within us.

In Romans 12:11, Paul also encourages us: "Be enthusiastic to serve the Lord, keeping your passion toward him boiling hot! Radiate with the glow of the Holy Spirit and let him fill you with excitement as you serve him" (TPT).

That's not all.

In being humble, we get to utilize our gifts effectively. We can honor the skills, accomplishments, and gifts God has given by acknowledging our dependence on God for them all (2 Cor. 3:5). We can do amazing things and show them off for His glory.

Writer Nellie Owens says, "God desires to be able to use us to His glory and for His purpose, and each of us should be aware of this. Humility is that we use our talents and capabilities under God's direction and leading, giving Him the honor and glory for what is accomplished in and through our lives."[4]

The Superpower of Submissiveness

Submissiveness is a curse word in our culture. But to God, it is a blessing. Psalm 37:11 assures us, "But the meek shall inherit the land and delight themselves in abundant peace" (ESV).

You probably balked at the word *meek*, but stay with me. I assure you, it's not what you think.

Meekness is often seen as weak and insignificant. Though the world has one definition, the Word has another. In a *Desiring God* article, Pastor John Piper says, "Meekness means committing your cause to God and not needing to defend yourself."[5]

Though this is a jam-packed term, I'll focus on the four points Piper mentions in the article.

Meek people believe in God. They trust He will come through for them. They understand their shortcomings and alleviate themselves of life's burdens by committing them to God. They wait on the Lord. They don't freak out; they understand God will move the most in their stillness. They're not concerned with their haters. Anger or resentment does not reside in them; they know God will not let His righteous be forsaken.

Moses was the greatest example of meekness. And might I argue, Joseph was too? You know, the colorful coat guy.

Though many recent commentaries consider Joseph arrogant in his youth, the Bible doesn't say he was prideful. I think he was just super excited about his gift and his divine dreams. In fact, even amid the atrocities he faced on his journey to becoming the most influential figure in Egypt, he held fast to his God-given dreams. Joseph further showed his humility when his brothers came crawling to his palace for help and he chose mercy instead of payback.

God's main goal wasn't to humble Joseph. But He did humble Joseph's brothers. They suffered, they repented, and they did, indeed, bow.

Maybe Joseph learned something too. Unless God gives you the go, don't be loud-mouthed about what He reveals to you.

Keep quiet until it's time. When it comes, He will lift you up, and you won't have to say a word about it.

Christlike confidence is a beautiful characteristic of God's heirs. When you bring humility into the mix, you're not dimming your light so someone around you can shine brighter. You're igniting the light of Christ so the world can see it wasn't your doing but His.

That is the wisdom of the meek. That is how you flourish in humility.

Therefore, if God's grace looks like an obnoxious, overpriced heart-shaped coat on you, so be it. With humility, just be sure to demonstrate to *everyone* that they can have this heart-shaped coat too.

Through Christ, it's free.

Kingdom Keys

- God envelops us *all* with a heart-shaped coat.
- When you're full of yourself, there's no room for God.
- Humility, submission, and meekness are rare qualities of strength.
- Have Christlike confidence! Your light will shine, and the world will see it's all about Him, not you.

Reflection: *In what areas of your life can you begin to be more humble?*

Ten

CHECK YOUR COURT

Ladies-in-Waiting

I sort of, maybe, binge-watched the four seasons of *Reign* in four days. Not four days consecutively, of course. It was so good, I needed to break away to gather my thoughts and also my heart. There were definitely some scenes that were necessary to skip (heads up, parents), but I got the gist of it. The history of the royals, that is.

In preparation for this book, I aimed to learn more about them. I'd been wanting to check out the CW series, and after watching just one episode, I committed to a Netflix plan. I'm not much of a television girl, so you must know that's like "official, official" for me.

Reign does a riveting job of depicting the lives of Mary, Queen of Scots and Queen Elizabeth I of England. From the set to the phenomenal costumes and story line, I was amazed by how well the production mimicked history. (An enhanced, dramatized, not-always-one-hundred-percent-accurate history.)

Aside from my newfound admiration for Mary, Queen of Scots, I was incredibly impressed by her ladies-in-waiting.

The role of a lady-in-waiting has been around for centuries, primarily in the royal family. Historically, the woman who occupied the prized position was of noble blood and was carefully chosen. The highest ladies-in-waiting of the privy chamber were the closest to the royals and were happily unpaid. Instead, they gained political power, grew in rank, and lived comfortably by their queen's side.[1]

Through history, ladies-in-waiting mostly assisted with correspondence and entertained visiting dignitaries. They also helped raise children, married into high station, created their own lines, and even took a bullet for the crown. The job has evolved over the years, with many of the assignments passed on to employees of the royals.

Today, the lady-in-waiting position still remains an integral part of the royal household, with that person functioning more as a secretary. However, their primary purpose remains true: to provide wise counsel and companionship.

"Friends" is what Queen Mary called hers.

When Mary was five years old, her mother sent her to be raised in France by the family of the dauphin—the future king of France she was to later wed—Francis II. She didn't go alone though. Mary's ladies left Scotland to wait on their queen.

Throughout the CW series, we see their love for their country, believing "Scotland over everything"—even in a foreign land. Their friendship was undeniably beautiful—we see them grow from young girls infatuated with romance and enjoying life at court into seemingly invincible women of wisdom and wit.

They honored their queen with their lives and were always present with a listening ear. They were voices of reason and were willing to sacrifice their own happiness to ensure their queen's successful reign.

Let us fast-forward to here, to now—to you. Queen, tell me, is that what your court looks like?

While you await reuniting with your Father in heaven, does your corner consist of a few women who believe "Christ over everything" while living in this foreign land? Do they honor you? Can you go to your girls for wise counsel? Are they willing to do all that's in their power to push you to a victorious life in Christ?

Often, the reason we find a gaping hole in our circles is because we have subscribed to the cultural ideations of friendship. We believe our bonds need to be about how the person is supposed to make us feel. Really, the Bible shows us true friendship is the result of being attentive to another's needs above our own. We are also quick to believe that if the relationship hits a rough patch, it must not be of God.

Author Christine Hoover puts it like this: "It sounds biblical to pursue idealistic unity and community. Friendship doesn't happen according to our dream world, however. . . . Friendship is formed between imperfect people among the concrete and messy realities of life."[2]

Hoover argues we mustn't turn away from the idea of friendship, just the belief that it will always be fun and that it will always feel good. She says, "When we hold an ideal of friendship in our minds, believing it's attainable, we hold a standard above the heads of real women God has placed in our lives, and then we wonder why we're constantly disappointed by the realities, complexities, and difficulties in our relationships."[3]

So how can we hold the proper standards for our friends? How can we be certain of who God has placed in our lives for us? How can we discern who needs to be in our courts?

Let us first look at God. After all, friendship was His idea. We see this through His companionship with His new creations in the garden of Eden, and even after sin corrupted our connection, God was actively pursuing ways to restore the relationship.

He chose Abraham as His friend and spoke to Moses face-to-face. They shared a close relationship, having the privilege to hear from God. In obedience, they led the way to the line of Christ.

Jesus Himself had disciples and made friends on His journey to the cross. At the Last Supper, He told His twelve disciples, "I'm no longer calling you servants because servants don't understand what their master is thinking and planning. No, I've named you friends because I've let you in on everything I've heard from the Father" (John 15:15 MSG).

Jesus giving up His own life on the cross is the greatest demonstration of friendship: "There is no greater love than to lay down one's life for one's friends" (John 15:13).

And now, as His living, breathing disciples today, Jesus calls us friends.

Covenant Friendships

God has set aside people who are meant to be your spiritual partners. There are God-sent friendships and there are covenant friendships—these are the people you are destined to do life with. God knows you need covenant friends for what He has called you to do.

It's imperative to be selective about who we surround ourselves with, as "bad company corrupts good character" (1 Cor. 15:33). What helped Heather Lindsey, founder of the Pinky Promise, in her walk with Christ was recognizing the three zones of friendships: the outer court, the inner court, and the Holy of Holies.[4]

The outer court consists of people you've known forever: perhaps your old college roommate, the woman you work with in ministry, the old friend you grew apart from, or the girl you met at summer camp who still likes your pictures on Instagram. In this court, they don't really know you. You are fond of one another but don't hold high expectations of each other. These aren't necessarily the ones you run to when you're down.

You can rely on your inner court more than your outer court friends. These are your close friends—you frequent one another's homes and often have a great time together. Some of your best friends may be sprinkled in there. And some may not be Christians. Regardless of their beliefs, they respect yours.

The closest to you is your Holy of Holies. In the Bible, the Holy of Holies was a sacred inner chamber that welcomed the presence of God. It was separated by a curtain from the outer chamber, and only the high priest was allowed in there. Before Christ died on the cross, which led to the curtain being torn in two, the Holy of Holies was the closest one could get to God.

Consider your Holy of Holies to be where your covenant husband and covenant friends can enter. These are the people who God has placed in your life to sacrificially push you toward Him and to encourage you in your purpose.

One of the most thoroughly depicted covenant friendships in the Bible is the one between David and Jonathan (1 Sam. 18:3).

When young shepherd David defeated Goliath and saved Israel, King Saul invited him to the palace. It was there he met the king's son, Jonathan, and they became fast friends. However, it's nothing like the kind of friendship we typically see. The English Standard Version of 1 Samuel 18:3 says, "Then Jonathan made a covenant with David, because he loved him as his own soul."

At first, King Saul welcomed David into his home. He was their country's newfound hero and his son's best friend, after all. However, Saul began to see David as a threat after his many military wins. David earned the love of the Israelites, and it stirred jealousy in the heart of Saul.

Saul actually had a lot to fear. Before David came along, Saul had dishonored God by breaking His commandment and making a sacrifice rather than waiting for Samuel, the prophet. Samuel had initially anointed Saul as king but now revealed God's plans to take away Saul's kingdom and present it to "a man after God's own heart" (1 Sam. 13:14). After that, Samuel anointed David to be the next king of Israel (1 Sam. 16:1–13). This happened before all of the jealousy—even before David stepped into Saul's life.

David knew his life was at risk. In the Message paraphrase of 1 Samuel 20:13–15, Jonathan promised him, "If my father still intends to kill you, I'll tell you and get you out of here. . . . And God be with you as he's been with my father!

If I make it through this alive, continue to be my covenant friend. And if I die, keep the covenant friendship with my family forever."

Even at David's weakest, Jonathan recognized the anointed power God had placed on David. Therefore, he did not promise to protect David's future throne. Instead, *he* asked for David's protection.

Jonathan went back home to reason with his father, and this time, the king hurled his spear to kill his own son.

Later, Jonathan told David that, indeed, the king was plotting murder. While saying their goodbyes, Jonathan blessed him, saying, "Go in peace, for we have sworn loyalty to each other in the LORD's name. The LORD is the witness of a bond between us and our children forever" (1 Sam. 20:42).

This is major, sis.

Jonathan conveyed his loyalty from a king—his own father—to David. He risked his life and gave up his legitimate claim to the throne. In turn, David vowed to protect Jonathan—his biggest contender for the throne. Going further, they made an oath to each other for life, solidifying a covenant for even their descendants.

This covenant friendship between Jonathan and David preserved the line of Christ. It illustrates the power of God and the covenant He has with us today. A friendship like theirs gives us a sneak peek of God's love we'll fully bask in when we get to heaven.

We don't have to shun friendship, compete, or live in isolation. We can navigate through this life with godly companionship. And with an example like the covenant friendship David and Jonathan had, we are able to learn how to be a friend ourselves. Proverbs 18:24 says, "There are 'friends' who destroy each other, but a real friend sticks closer than a brother."

Or in our case, a sister!

Though covenant friendships aren't feasible with every friend in your outer or inner court, God will still give you someone to look out for, and she will look after you.

Friendship on a Firm Foundation

David and Jonathan teach us many things.

A covenant friendship is loving your sister as you love yourself. A covenant friend realizes how great your future is in the Lord and aims to protect and honor you. A covenant friend doesn't fight for a gift God has given you, even if it puts you in the spotlight and moves them to the shadows. A covenant friendship breeds generations and generations of blessings.

We know all friendships won't be covenant. However, as daughters of the King, one factor we must consider when appointing our inner courts is a friend's position with Christ.

The surest way to know if we have built godly friendships is to discover whether our friends are bringing us closer to Jesus, and vice versa. With this as the proper and only firm foundation, godly characteristics stream into the lives of your court friends and into your own.

Sometimes we're called to be the Jonathan to a David.

Jonathan challenges us to be a better friend. He fostered a spiritual bond. He was a protector and encourager, and he harbored no jealousy. He kept David's distress confidential, and like Christ, he demonstrated sacrificial love. These are all the traits we should be able to pour into the David of our lives.

Then there are times when God places us in the life of a friend He just wants us to love on. Our role is to pour into her the love of Christ.

However, it is at all times that we are to help our sisters—whether they are believers or not.

Completely heartbroken over the final scenes of *Reign*, I cancelled my Netflix subscription and headed to the internet to study what was true and what was not. Before I go further, do understand that nothing I share is spoilers—this is world history!

The scenes showed Mary, Queen of Scots writing a letter to her cousin, Queen Elizabeth I of England, after Scotland forced her to abdicate. A prisoner in her own country, she fled to England in hope of Elizabeth's open heart, but life was worse there.

Fearful Mary would take her throne, Elizabeth imprisoned Mary for eighteen years. On top of that, she chopped her head off when supposed evidence of assassination conspiracies surfaced. Researching history, I was disappointed to discover that, indeed, all of this truly happened. Queen Elizabeth refused to help her cousin in real life. And not only that, in the eighteen years of imprisoning her, the queen never even met her.

Though they weren't in one another's court, they shared royal blood. However, society bred them to grow up in fear of being replaced by each other, so comparison and competitiveness were ingrained in Elizabeth's mind. Mary, on the other hand, desperately believed in the support of a woman in a world where men sought to take their lives.

But Elizabeth kept Mary hidden away in order to protect herself, and then she had her executed—she allowed society to pit her against her sister.

For weeks, I kept imagining what if. What if Queen Elizabeth had helped Queen Mary? It's idealistic of me considering their political climate, but perhaps the two queens could've worked side by side for the good of both of their nations. What if they had helped each other? What would the political relationship between the two countries look like today if they had?

What if *we* helped one another?

I can't help but think about how many times we leave our sisters to fend for themselves, or maybe even kick them when they're down, out of pride and self-preservation. How often do we knock the crowns off our fellow queens in order to ensure a lasting rule for ourselves? To ensure everyone loves us, not her? Or to assure ourselves that we are "better" than her?

The reality is this: as sisters in Christ, we have one common goal. The world may try to twist our stories, they may try to pit us against one another, they will try to make us unnecessary enemies. But the outcome will be beautiful should we band together for the sake of God's kingdom.

There is so much power in the fellowship of women. The world realizes that and aims to keep us divided whether it be through reality television or drama in our own churches. We can rise up and stand undefeated together. The New International Version of Ecclesiastes 4:12 says, "Though one may be overpowered, two can defend themselves. A cord of three strands is not quickly broken."

We mustn't be disingenuous in support of our sisters. We mustn't grudgingly help or be good Samaritans under false pretenses. We mustn't be like Job's friends, who thought they had all the knowledge as to why he was suffering and persecuted him when he actually had done nothing wrong (Job 32:1–37:24).

We must check our courts, but we must also check ourselves. We can only earnestly defend our sister if we take inventory from where we sit on our thrones.

In a sermon series based on the ministry of family, Dr. Matthew Stevenson said, "Half daughters cannot be whole sisters."[5] We are queens at ruining relationships because we become incomplete when we choose to listen to Satan's voice instead of God's. What he doesn't tell you is that if you allow your fears and insecurities to reign over your relationships, you, like Queen Elizabeth I, sign up for a lifetime of loneliness.

Being vulnerable is a dangerous and sometimes scary condition. You will get burned. But healing does come. There will be times when you will be misunderstood and experience betrayal like none other. But there are women who genuinely desire to rule together.

There are women who are trustworthy, who will love you at all times (Prov. 17:17), lift you up (Eccles. 4:10), alleviate your burdens (Gal. 6:2), edify you (Prov. 27:6), lovingly tell the truth even when you don't want to hear it (Matt. 18:15), and believe you are worth the sacrifice (Phil. 2:3).

These friends will become mouthpieces for God to encourage you—taking you for a much-needed night out, sending you a care package to campus after you fail a test, and dropping an Edible Arrangements gift at your door after a breakup.

Instead of strategizing payback, will your girls seek out prayer time? Are they similar to the group in the Bible who lowered their friend, a paraplegic, down from the roof to get past the crowds and straight to Jesus's healing hand (Mark 2:1–12)? Do your friends carry you to your miracle?

Like the baby who leaped in Elizabeth's womb upon hearing Mary's voice, do your friends jump for joy at the sound of something new birthing inside of you (Luke 1:41)?

Like the loyalty demonstrated between a mother and daughter-in-law, Ruth and Naomi, do your friendships promise a devoted love (Ruth 1:16–17)?

If so, thank Jesus.

As writer Rachel Lehner says, when we ask the Lord and He delivers a godly friend into our lives, "it should draw our hearts to thank him for the dearest friend of all, Jesus. His victory over death made him the firstborn of many brothers and sisters who will one day be together, sinless, in perfect unity and love."[6]

Together, we can mirror the girl gang of Marys who tirelessly journeyed to get to Jesus's burial site, determined to honor Him with fragrances and oils. With Christ, we don't have to be ladies who wait but can be ladies who rise to the occasion and get to work. Through our love and unification, we can be the glimpse of heaven that people come across on this earth.

Kingdom Keys

- Not all friendships will be covenant.
- God has set aside people who are meant to be your spiritual partners. He knows you need your covenant friends for what He has called you to do.

- A covenant friendship is loving your sister as you love yourself. A covenant friend will realize how great your future is in the Lord; they aim to protect and honor you. A covenant friend doesn't fight for gifts God has given you, even if it puts you in the spotlight and moves them to the shadows. A covenant friendship breeds generations and generations of blessings.
- The outcome will be beautiful should women band together for the sake of God's kingdom.

Reflection: *Has God given you a godly friendship? Text your friend right now and show her some love! If you don't have one yet, pray for a friend like that, and join the Adorned in Armor Community Facebook group. You might find her there!*

Eleven

SECURE YOUR PALACE

We live in the era of believing we are "strong enough" to handle seeing certain things, listening to certain things, and allowing certain things into our space. We indulge, we entertain, we play with fire because we think, when it's time, we will have the power to say, "Enough is enough." We believe we can escape these situations unscathed.

The world made us think that way. We're told to wear our hearts on our sleeves but also to protect our hearts. We've been convinced we are in control. God tells us to protect our hearts too but for entirely different reasons. In Proverbs 4:23, we are told to guard our hearts before anything because our hearts direct where we will go in life.

I argue that our hearts are still at risk because we're guarding ourselves from the wrong things. We might consider the only culprit to be the man who won't be true to us. We often think what God meant is that we need to be "good people." But God isn't calling us to be good; He's calling us to be holy.

What if I told you the walls you created to protect yourself have long crumbled down? What if I told you the culprit was already inside? That the intruder has made it past your defenses and has already made your heart his throne?

Take this as your security alert: your palace has been invaded, and it's time to detect what dared enter. Welcomed or not, it is time to drag it out, kicking and screaming.

First, let's identify: What have you allowed inside your heart?

> Now the practices of the sinful nature are clearly evident: they are sexual immorality, impurity, sensuality (total irresponsibility, lack of self-control), idolatry, sorcery, hostility, strife, jealousy, fits of anger, disputes, dissensions, factions [that promote heresies], envy, drunkenness, riotous behavior, and other things like these. I warn you beforehand, just as I did previously, that those who practice such things will not inherit the kingdom of God. (Gal. 5:19–21 AMP)

Yeah, I know. My eyes got wide and my heart skipped too. We're in dire need of extra precaution, sis. In choosing to indulge sin without repentance, we choose life on earth but an eternity locked outside the palace we were once promised.

You probably sighed in relief at some of the more blatant sins, thinking you were off the hook. And so I'd like to focus on the one we often immediately check off as unrelatable. It is one of the most practiced sins today, because we don't know we have committed it. It is the sin of idolatry.

The Israelites knew exactly what they were doing. Worried their leader Moses wouldn't return from his trek up Mount Sinai, they gathered around Aaron to implore him, "Make us some gods who can lead us" (Exod. 32:1).

Somehow they forgot God granted them freedom from Egypt and even parted the Red Sea to solidify their escape. They chose to worship a golden calf they created with their own hands instead. Through the faithlessness of the Israelites, we see how when we forget who God is to us, we easily succumb to sin.

We also witness how the human heart desires lordship. We want something to reign over us. We want something to live for, to give us direction, inspiration, hope. And so we search for it in other things.

Our "things" have evolved; our worship is different. We may not be sacrificing animals and bowing before objects. We may not be setting our gold earrings ablaze, preparing our molten calf, but we have created our own idols in different ways.

Idolatry, we think, refers to those who are worshiping celebrities. However, that's not the only form of idol worship. Anything (even church) can become a form of idolatry!

- If you cannot go a moment without checking your reflection in an object—is that your idol?
- If you devote every night to binge-watching your favorite shows—is that your idol?

- If social media is the first thing you reach for before starting your day—if "likes" and comments are what fuel you throughout each day—is that your idol?

Loving yourself is beautiful, entertainment is a great enhancement to one's day, and social media is a great tool. So no, these things aren't bad in themselves. They only become your idols when your devotions take you away from God. It's when they come first that they become a problem. As for church, God desires that we enthusiastically serve and fellowship, but idol worship comes into play when our worship becomes a performance rather than an act of praise.

When I first listened to Jimmy Needham's recording of "Clear the Stage," I got goosebumps. The artist sings about getting rid of everything to give God glory. The lyrics take us on a journey through all the things vying for our attention: our own plans, friends, the world, church. He encourages doing whatever is necessary so we can worship with our lives and not just with our mouths.

An idol is anything we place before our one true God. It's whatever we're constantly thinking of. It's whatever we're devoting our minds, our hearts to. The Message version of Jonah 2:8 says when we worship "god-frauds," we're walking away from our only true love.

Can you imagine that? Becoming so infatuated with something else—something we pursue endlessly with no reciprocal feelings—that we neglect the love God has consistently lavished upon us before we were even in our mother's womb? That is what we do.

God isn't just heartbroken over our betrayal; He's righteously angry. In fact, He refers to Himself as a "jealous God."

What in the world does God, the Creator of the universe, have to be jealous about?

It's us! The jealousy God attributes to Himself isn't the sin we're so familiar with. He doesn't play around with His name *or* His namesake:

> In His infinite holiness, God is supremely dedicated to preserving His honor with exclusive devotion and worship. To require less would relegate Him to a lesser position of glory. "I, the LORD, am the one, and I won't give my name and glory to another, nor my praise to idols" (Isa. 42:8). This aspect of jealousy indicates God's holy zeal for the honor of His name and the good of those who are bound to Him in a covenant relationship (Ezek. 39:23–25).[1]

You see that? God's jealousy is synonymous with "holy zeal"—it is not motivated by the jealousy the Bible warns us about. Insecurity, pride, spite, and evil have no relation to God. When He says He is jealous for you, that is reason for His people to praise Him and for His enemies to fear Him. Bible.org says, "God is zealous—eager about protecting what is precious to Him."[2]

Our God in heaven desires relationships with us so that we aren't tainted by this world, its idols, and, ultimately, Satan. Knowing this, Satan works hard to find the very things we love to influence us to do his will. He pays attention to our weaknesses and employs them as his own power to pull us away from God. He aids us in formulating our own idols because that form of worship goes to him.

Damage control is possible. Here are the types of behavior to look out for when it comes to guarding our hearts from idolatry:

- Entertaining things God wouldn't approve of because we can go apologize later. It's "not a big deal."
- "Halfway" sins. We think we're maintaining our purity by not going all the way.
- Believing we have the power to erase the habit out of our memory.

When we submit to these behaviors, they lead us to betray our King. We let idols in by not obeying God's commandments and committing the blatant sins, and then the secret sins we don't talk about. Any sin.

This is why it's important to pay close attention to guarding our eyes because they lead to the heart. Often we are too lenient with the things we consume: from movies to music, we watch and listen as if dirty lyrics and inappropriate scenes can't seep into our spirits. Luke 11:34 says, "Your eye is like a lamp that provides light for your body. When your eye is healthy, your whole body is filled with light. But when it is unhealthy, your body is filled with darkness."

Regardless of what the idol is—clothes, makeup, work, money, school, your blessings, your man (even a godly one)—you have dethroned your one true King. John Piper says, "Whatever lures your affections away from God with deceptive attraction will come back to strip you bare and cut you in pieces."[3]

We all need help. We don't have *any* power apart from Christ. Whether or not we willingly allow these idols entry to our hearts, there is still hope for us. All we need is Christ.

It's time to identify our idols and give God His rightful place. The things we worship are worthless. Your heart is your palace with a throne only fit for the King of all kings—the only invincible, incomparable God. Protect it in preparation for your palace in heaven.

Kingdom Keys

- Take inventory of what is on the throne of your heart. We can't allow our sins to take root and live comfortably in our palaces.
- God wants our whole hearts, not the piece we left for Him *after* everything else has had its fill.
- God will not condemn you for what you struggle with. He will redeem you and will always be the King of your heart if you first make room for Him.

Reflection: *What or who has your full attention? Has time with them taken God's place?*

Twelve

AMPLIFYING YOUR VOICE

Satan has been trying to stifle my voice since birth.

At nine o'clock on an unnaturally warm night in October, my mom began feeling contractions. Being a nurse, she didn't fret or rush to the hospital; she knew it wasn't time to deliver. Through grimaces and squirming, she entertained guests at home instead. When they left, she rested, awaiting my arrival. The expected date for my birth was that day, the 24th.

The pain became unbearable at one o'clock in the morning—she was officially in labor. My father, my mom's favorite aunt, and my mom's sister situated her in the car and raced to the hospital. There they waited hours for her cervix to dilate. After what seemed like forever, it finally did.

Once her cervix was fully dilated, Mom did her best to push me out. After two exhausting hours, she stopped pushing. She was already weak from mourning because she'd laid her father to rest only two days before.

And then the obstetrician shared that my umbilical cord was wrapped around my neck. Though a natural occurrence, he feared it was too tight. He had only just seen the sign of it on the fetal ultrasound machine.

"Please, Maggie. Please push," the obstetrician said. Everyone in the room repeated their own renditions after him. My father, a wide-eyed mess. My great-aunt, goading her through the pain.

I began to crown.

Taking a peek, the doctor announced that the cord around my neck was indeed nearly suffocating me and that my mom would have to push harder.

My mother mustered the little strength she had left and with one last push, she gave birth to me. After more than ten hours of labor, I let out a scream that rivaled a baby elephant's trumpet.

The obstetrician clamped and cut the cord. I was free. No complications, completely healthy.

My mom has told me that story over and over, but it wasn't until recently that I began to ponder how I found my voice. I've mentioned it before, but I was super shy growing up. My mom always shares how shocked she is at who I am today, and I always laugh in agreement.

My shyness was so bad that corny adults would ask, "Cat got your tongue?" almost every day of my kid life. I also didn't like people much . . . unless we're talking family.

In elementary school, I was afraid to draw attention to myself. I made great friends, but I don't recall making the first move. In middle school, I was still shy, but my style started to speak for me. My quietness then had less to do with fear and more to do with "not feeling like" speaking. I was myself with my friends, laughing boisterously. However, outside of that, I'd only smile my hellos and speak when spoken to.

In high school, I busted out of my shell. I wasn't a whole new person . . . I just let who I was on the inside come out. My favorite English teacher wrote in my yearbook, "Find your voice and share it with the world."

In college, I did just that. In those four years, my main concern was making sure my thoughts and feelings were heard. I realized the importance of speaking up.

I'm certain Ariel did too. I came across a Disney theory video about why the little mermaid's voice was so important. First, it was passed down from her mother. Second, everyone was fascinated with her sound. She captivated with her voice and used her influence to restore environments. Under the sea, she brought the ocean creatures together, ending discord and the effects of evil.

Ursula didn't just desire Ariel's voice to conceal her identity from the prince. Ursula wasn't as powerful as she put on; she needed Ariel's voice in order to reign supreme. When Ariel sacrificed her voice to get rid of her mermaid tail and find love, she gave away her true power and lost the ability to communicate who she really was.

When we don't speak, decisions are made for us. When we don't speak, we rob ourselves of protection. When we don't speak, we rob others of getting to know us. But when we speak up, we own ourselves, giving glory to God by being who we were created to be.

I love being audacious, and I take pride in my boldness, especially when considering where I came from. I am still rather shy at times, but I understand the weight of who I am and I walk purposefully in it. To my quiet ones out there, you can be soft-spoken with a commanding presence. There's more harm in silence than in speaking up.

Using Our Voices

One thing I always spoke out about was my faith in Jesus. No, I wouldn't let the enemy put a clamp over my mouth. I was a bold believer who wouldn't stand for blasphemy against my God, even if I only uttered one sentence to shut it down. The more I pursued Christ, the more our relationship trickled audaciousness into every area of my life.

In the process, He showed me that He gave me the gift of encouragement. I would say I inherited it from my mother, who is perhaps my World's Biggest Cheerleader, but I recall from my very limited knowledge of science that those kinds of traits aren't passed on. So I'll say it comes naturally and is something I genuinely enjoy doing.

God planted the desire in me to leave people with the feeling that everything was going to be okay. I was the one people would approach to have their spirits lifted. And when I wasn't speaking encouragement, I was writing it.

Before my blog, I was writing inspirational poems and essays in elementary and middle school. In high school, I'd pick Scripture to study and would send notes to all of my friends—Christian or not—about what I learned and how we could apply it. Sometimes God would even put someone's name on my heart, urging me to send them a message He intended for them or to simply say, "I love you."

In college, I frequented our filming studio to rent their cameras. Many nights I would stay up late creating content; I began performing spoken-word poetry. Thus began my love for speaking out God's messages on a new level. My channel's banner read, "Luke 6:45—For the mouth speaks what the heart is full of."

Praise was what was on my lips. According to Proverbs 18:21, the power of life and death lies in the tongue, and I desired to use that power to speak life.

Negative Words

I'm far from perfect and would never act as if nothing negative has left my mouth. I can remember times when I'd curse in anger or accidentally rap the curses in the latest hit song. At one point, I found myself slipping and not thinking anything of it. But James 3:10 reads, "Out of the same mouth we pour out words of praise one minute and curses the next. My brothers and sisters, this should never be!" (TPT).

It's impossible to have negative, derogative speech on the very same lips we use to give our God the glory. Curses cancel out our praise. In fact, they render our religion pointless (James 1:26).

We're urged to understand that we should not only listen to God's Word but also actually follow it. If we don't, we're only playing ourselves. The Bible compares this foolishness to looking at a mirror and walking away, completely forgetting what we look like.

Lies

Lying is included as well. Lying only plans destruction (Ps. 52:2), recklessly pierces like a sword (Prov. 12:18), crushes spirits (Prov. 15:4), and cuts down life (Prov. 12:19).

In Psalm 34:13, we're warned to keep our tongues from evil and our lips from telling lies. Yes, even the ones you think will protect yourself or someone you care about. No, small white lies aren't as small as they seem. The Bible uses strong words, explaining that God *hates* lies, period. Detests them, even (Prov. 6:16–19). He considers them an abomination (Prov. 12:22).

Gossip

Our hearts can easily be corrupted. So we're warned to flee from all negative talk—including the culprit gossip. Our society glorifies it. Our circles may breed it. Our lives may be ruined by it.

There are books and TV shows with gossip as the foundation. (Anyone else used to sign out with "xoxo, Gossip Girl"?) It's in the media; it's in real life, and men and women both do it. Gossiping is easy to slip into and an experience we've all been exposed to, whether you were in the group chat on the receiving end or you were the one Facetiming your girls to spread it.

It's human nature to enjoy gossip. Proverbs 18:8 tells us: "The words of a gossip are swallowed greedily, and they go down into a person's innermost being" (GW). We desire it—swallowing it not in small pieces but in mouth-salivating chunks, filling everything in our bodies but bringing malnourishment to our souls. Indeed, gossip is food, but that doesn't mean it's good.

When we gossip, we are considered "godless" (2 Tim. 2:16). When we gossip, we are toxic, poisoning the body of believers

(James 3:8). When we gossip, we are an endangerment to our own lives as well as our friends.

The Bible says gossipers cannot be trusted. The Word says to get out to salvage your life (Prov. 20:19).

Engaging in any corrupt talk brings about nothing but trouble. It results in hatred, strife, and bitterness. It feeds our flesh, leaving us with the craving for more and more attention. It thrives on building us up as we bulldoze others. It eradicates the seriousness of the sin, causing us to fall deeper and deeper into selfishness, insecurity, and destructive carelessness.

In Proverbs 21:23, however, we're told that when we avoid all corrupt speech, we avoid calamity. Surrendering our desire for idle chatter to God will switch out dead words for resurrecting life. We, instead, will be able to use that power to breathe serenity into a room. Like the obstetrician, we must clamp and cut the cord of sin that so easily entangles us.

Restraint Is Power

It's time to get serious with the words that come out of our mouths. According to Matthew 12:37, our words will either justify or condemn us. And as a naturally quiet woman, I'd say the simplest way to escape hateful speech is to hold your tongue. Proverbs 17:27–28 agrees: "The one who has knowledge uses words with restraint, and whoever has understanding is even-tempered. Even fools are thought wise if they keep silent, and discerning if they hold their tongues" (NIV).

We must store up God's Word in our hearts because only then will we find wisdom. This is not something we can do on our own. The Holy Spirit renews us and helps us with this.

The longest psalm and longest chapter in the Bible, Psalm 119, is evidence of this. The passage praises God and His Holy Word, referencing Scripture 171 times out of 176 verses! The writer clearly saw how important it was to fill his heart with the Word so that good things flowed from his mouth.

Delight in God's Word; indulge in it. It is not enough to do anything less; there's nothing we can do that would mean more. We are to be walking lights of Christ, uplifting the body and preaching to the world of God's goodness.

You too can be an encourager. In Ephesians 4:29, we discover that we are to speak only "what is helpful for building others up according to their needs" so we can "benefit those who listen" (NIV). But the only way to spread the message of encouragement is to first serve an eviction notice to unwholesome talk.

So then, neglect negative words and flee from lies and gossip—instead, spread the gospel. Whisper no harmful talk—instead, shout hope. Tell the world about the good news of Jesus Christ, spreading His light and love to all you come across.

Speak Life

My mother can't stand to see me upset, so whenever I'm down, she retells the story of my birth. She reminds me, "You bring the family joy." She speaks of how even in that bleak time of losing her father, she felt the solace of bringing a child into the world. Everyone was reminded of hope; everyone just wanted to hold the baby.

So while visitors came to the house to give both their condolences and their congratulations, the birth of a tiny human alleviated some of the pain. All of my aunts, my uncles, my cousins, and my grandmother—they still missed my grandfather. But God granted them a blessing in their bleeding: the cries of an infant, a reminder that new life was there.

And so I say to you, you bring this dismal world *joy*. You are not too small to have an impact. Your presence and your voice—they matter. Satan is well aware of this and will try to stifle your influence. He will try to dirty your heart so that you vomit words of destruction.

But what you cradle within you contains life. You embody encouragement when you take on the joy of salvation and use your lips to bring hope into darkness.

Kingdom Keys

- The devil is afraid of what God can do through and with you.
- Remember the power of what you say. It speaks either life or death.
- You can't curse people and praise God with the same lips.
- The world needs your voice.

Reflection: *What is one way you can encourage someone today?*

MORE THAN ENOUGH

I felt like a loser when I didn't get a job after college. I mean, I knew I wasn't, but I *felt* like one.

A loss of hope wasn't my issue. God knew how much I needed a job, how much I needed to help my family. I wholeheartedly believed He would come through for me. I believed He would honor me as I diligently worked hard in school all my life.

When I received my Who's Who plaque, my parents didn't worry about what I would become.

When my school announced I was graduating summa cum laude, we didn't focus on where that status would take me.

When I walked across that stage with six tassels of honor around my neck and the loving cheers of my family around me, we had no worries about my leaving college without a form of consistent income.

Surely, sooner or later I would obtain a job I desired . . . right?

I knew the job market was rough, so I waited patiently. Then the months flew by and I began to question. I wondered why my job was taking so long to get to me. I did all the right things: made the right connections, landed the right internships and shadowing opportunities.

And yet, there I was. Home.

I was working on my brand, but it felt like I was doing absolutely nothing. Everything felt like nothing. Nothing, because I was so accustomed to getting up and getting to work. Nothing, because there wasn't anything I could do about it. Nothing, because I didn't have a pervasive mission to accomplish. With that absent, I felt blah. I was waiting on my job in the real world. Because I didn't have it, I often found myself feeling inadequate. There's no better way to explain the feeling than with this narration.

Are you ready?

There's this episode of *SpongeBob SquarePants* I'm always reminded of (yes, I just went there). It's the one where his idol ties him on two sticks and gives him a horn to blow in lieu of catching a queen jellyfish.

Have you ever watched that episode? The horn made a sound that cried "loser" every time SpongeBob blew into it. Pretty funny stuff.

If you haven't seen it, let us revisit my childhood for a bit.

SpongeBob and Patrick were attending a biannual jellyfish convention when SpongeBob spotted his idol. His name was Kevin, and he was the leader of Bikini Bottom's premier jellyfish enthusiast club—and also . . . a cucumber born with a crown.

Like us, Patrick didn't see what the big deal was about a "nerdy pickle." SpongeBob attempted to explain how awesome Kevin was. He said, "If I could just touch the hem of his pocket protector, then maybe some of his greatness would rub off on me."

SpongeBob stalked Kevin for the rest of the episode until Kevin gave him an opportunity to join the insiders' club. First, SpongeBob would have to complete a series of ridiculously rigorous tests. SpongeBob, being the big fan that he was, wanted the position so badly he did whatever was required.

In the end, SpongeBob discovered the queen jellyfish mission was a fraud and so was Kevin. Embarrassed and disappointed, he laid down being the "biggest fan." He realized he didn't need to get into the club; he'd much rather be himself.

Crazy, but this episode of *SpongeBob* reminded me of a story in the Bible. There was once an outcast, a woman who suffered from constant bleeding for twelve years. She came up behind Jesus and touched the hem of His robe, believing, "If I can just touch his robe, I will be healed" (Matt. 9:21).

Unlike Kevin, there's nothing fake about Jesus. In a crowd full of people, Jesus turned and caught sight of her. He spoke to her, and she was healed at that very moment (v. 22).

Maybe your issue isn't obviously external, such as bleeding. Maybe it's something you find inside yourself. Maybe you fight the feeling of inferiority.

Do you have the tendency to say yes to everything? Or, are you inclined to look at yourself through the lens of labels, as I did?

God has healed us from being outsiders, from settling for the titles the world gives us, from being fans of the hustle. We don't have to work hard to attain a label—God has called us His children!

We are more than our achievements and more than what we have not accomplished. Our worth isn't based on what we do but on who we are.

It's human nature to label ourselves and others. Because we are shaped by this world, we tend to identify people by what they do rather than who they are. We categorize them based on their professions or their standing in life. We group one another with labels, building unnecessary hierarchies. We attach a certain amount of value to each title, and often our hyper-obsessions unconsciously prompt us to go for more. We use everything from simple introductions to hashtags or strategically filled social media biographies so that people can see our labels.

However, the label a job brings doesn't elevate us. God does. We have to know who God says we are outside of everything else.

All the accolades don't mean a thing if we are hoping to catch our identity outside of Jesus. All the shiny rewards and status boosters are nice, but they are meaningless in the eyes of Christ.

And I *knew* this, but I had to experience it to fully understand.

When I was jobless, I found I was putting a lot of stock in what I did and accomplished. I made these things my identity. I realized the reason I felt "nothingness" was because I was basing my purpose on roles that meant nothing. All God wanted me to be was myself.

All He wants you to be is yourself.

And that means not stretching yourself thin in the chase but committing yourself to accomplish the things God tells you to do. Jesus took that advice to the grave!

In John 5:19, Jesus explained, "I tell you the truth, the Son can do nothing by himself. He does only what he sees the Father doing. Whatever the Father does, the Son also does."

When you do the work of our Father, you can say "enough is enough" to everything else. I'm not saying it'll be easy. In this digital age, it will especially be a fight.

I learned a very important lesson in joblessness: Jesus wanted me to chuck my checklist and be still. He wanted to show me He was God. You may think you are positioning yourself for your best life, but we are not the ones orchestrating our future. Ambition is great and is needed for kingdom work, but don't let it make you think you need to be doing more when God is telling you to rest.

If you're a self-sufficient type like me, you'll find that God will want to surprise people like us the most. It'll put you in shock, but it's a necessary humbling. Realizing there's nothing you can do is the best position to occupy.

There's nothing you can be but His child. It's an honor knowing who we are is enough.

Being an heir to the kingdom is more than enough.

A castle's kitchen boy fell in love with a girl of noble blood.

He pursued her, and though the girl knew their relationship could go nowhere, she finally relented. She was beginning to feel the same way.

Still, she often reminded the boy of the impending doom: her parents disowning her and him losing his job. She half-heartedly tried to end the relationship herself.

The boy didn't want to let her go. He promised their love was enough. He promised they could live a much happier, simpler life. And when that didn't work, he promised he would rise in rank for her. He went to war for her.

Literally.

And while at war, he fought victoriously and won favor in the sight of the king. The boy kept his promise—he was granted land and rose in station, the very first of his family to break the cycle.

But when he returned, he found it was too late. The noble girl was still undeniably in love with him, but her family had arranged for her to be married off to a wealthy suitor. She refused to say goodbye to a life of stability.

Heartbroken, the soldier remained in the castle and fulfilled his duties by the king's side.

Then the king's little sister came home. The queen decided she needed someone to keep the young princess at bay from noblemen and ordered the soldier to become her guard.

And guess what?

He fell in love with her too.

It was a reciprocated love but still hopeless from the outside. She was royalty, after all. This time around, the princess desperately wanted to marry the soldier.

And this time, they both made promises. She promised she would ask her brother, the king, to make him a duke. He promised he would do whatever it took to marry her. She promised she would wait.

But she didn't.

When the guard returned from his duties outside of the castle, he found the princess wed. This time they both were heartbroken, as the princess had been led to believe he was dead. Tragically, they mourned the loss of their future together. He left the castle and eventually found love with a village girl.

A sucker for romance, I was initially rooting for the kitchen boy turned soldier turned guard. But after a while I grew exasperated with him, thinking, *Didn't he learn his lesson the first time? This is a princess we're talking about—society, let alone the crown, will not allow it!*

The poor man had good intentions but became engrossed with the prize to the point it ruled over him. He became willing to do just about anything to attain it. He became consumed with wanting to be bigger, to be . . . somebody. And still, there was always an extra step to take.

I began to think of this hopeless situation in light of our own pursuits of "becoming somebody."

Would you call social media your forbidden love?

As much as we'd like to think social media doesn't influence us, statistics prove otherwise. It affects our world. It challenges us to chase.

Do you find yourself chasing for worth through Women Crush Wednesdays? Are you labeling yourself based on the number of likes you receive? Are you in constant pursuit of the *k* on Instagram?

It's a natural feeling to want to be liked, needed, loved. But when we obsessively set our eyes on these goals, they lead to a dead end. Like the kitchen boy turned castle guard, we'll see that when we go through all the necessary and even absurd measures, we still end up dissatisfied.

The object of our chase isn't bad in itself. It's the motive behind it. Why do you need to post this very picture? Why Facetune your body shape? What will the blue check on Instagram do for you personally?

A sure method to spot the ways social media negatively influences you is to measure how you feel when you're using it and when you are not. The biggest factor is when you begin to compare yourself to others.

You were fine when you signed into the app, but all of a sudden you feel you have to play catch-up and post a photo as equally cute as one posted by that celebrity you love. You were content taking classes at a community college until you saw your rival shared her acceptance into the Ivy League. You were happily celebrating your singleness at a girls' night out until you scrolled past the girl with the engagement ring.

Comparison causes you to doubt yourself and neglect the blessings you already have. It encourages you to partake in activity you typically wouldn't just because it's "in" right now. It prods you to polish your digital persona and neglect your heart. It makes you feel you've been left behind in your journey to "leveling up."

If we're not careful, jealousy will rot us from within and expose itself in our speech and actions. It's important to maintain healthy boundaries and exercise caution so we don't fall victim to the aimless pursuit of validation.

Often, this pursuit is difficult to see until it's too late because this world promises a lot of things. If you work hard, you will be rich. If you look a certain way, you will get the perfect guy. If you go viral, everyone will love you. But what good is it to gain the love of the whole world and lose yourself (Matt. 16:26)?

We're chasing the wrong thing. Christ is clout. He may seem unpopular on social media, in your circles, in your world. But when you chase Him, you'll find your true value.

Will you attempt all the latest trends to remain relevant? Will you do all you can to have someone comment #goals under your photo? Or will you rest in the satisfaction of what salvation did for your soul?

If you choose the latter, you'll quickly discover that yes, you *can* level up in rank. The highest tier in life is "child of God."

Kingdom Keys

- You are validated by God—not titles, status, position, or social media. Accolades don't mean a thing if you are hoping to catch your identity outside of Jesus.
- God will strip you of all the excess to allow you to see you are more than enough in Him. You lack nothing.
- Comparison destroys—minding the business of others limits how you view the way God has blessed you.
- Attempting to remain relevant in a culture that is always on to the next thing will leave you running on empty.

Reflection: *What label have you been chasing? Why?*

PATIENCE IS A VIRTUE

The most ridiculous commercial was released while I was in eighth grade. I'm not exaggerating when I say it came on in between and at the end of every show. I don't think we had the ability to fast-forward commercials then. Or maybe my brother lost the remote.

We would either watch the commercials or go on a bathroom break or snack run to pass the time. This particular commercial, however, was worth staying around for. It was an advertisement in which a whole bunch of random people angrily screamed out their window, "It's my money and I need it now!"

Google it. It was incredibly corny, and you just had to laugh. Whether I was at school or at home, there would be that one person screaming at the top of their lungs, making a mockery out of the actors. We would even have contests to see who could do it best.

Whenever I think of patience, that commercial is the first thing that comes to mind. Though inadvertently, I think the advertisement fairly depicts us in this instant-gratification society of ours.

We want our degree now, our dream job now, our man now, our wedding and riches and kids now. We want all of our blessings now, now, now. Or we at least need a preview.

My parents needed one too. The preview, I mean. But in a different way. They are sincerely invested in the lives of my siblings and me, so they often check in to see where our heads are.

When you live in a Caribbean household, the conversation of education and careers is always on your lips. I remember having a great conversation with my dad my senior year of college. It was the kind where you figure out future plans together—a pleasant father-daughter convo in which I explained how I was aiming to "get my life."

I had no worries then. Surely, I would get a job.

As I mentioned earlier, I didn't.

In a more eloquent manner, my father explained that "it's real out here" in the job market and that I should go back to school to beat out my competitors. When I told him my dream entry-level job was to work at *Teen Vogue*, he encouraged me to go for it, but he also advised me to take a professional job anywhere else in communications to work my way up.

He argued that at least I'd get my feet wet and be more exposed to the job I actually wanted. I have absolutely no problem working my way up. I know how it is to be at the bottom. But though he was right, I couldn't find myself saying yes to a job that was the complete opposite of me.

Is this a millennial thing? Was I being picky? Was it wrong to say no to other jobs just because I wanted to be happy there? Because I wanted to be *led* there?

Perhaps. But I knew then, and I know now: it's not pickiness; it's about peace. I don't want to say yes if I feel God is telling me, "No, hold on."

And so, I waited.

Working retail granted me the freedom to grow my brand and shop great discounted deals. However, as mentioned, I would find myself feeling "off" because I was not where I wanted to be. I remember thinking, *God, hurry this process up!*

He has slowly molded me over the years, so I've gotten way better with patience, but let me tell you, it never used to be my strong suit. I've always been fairly patient with people. However, when it came to getting what I want? Let's just say, I want my money and I want it now.

And then *something* finally happened.

Several months after college graduation, I got invited to an event hosted by a radio show. I don't even listen to the radio, but somehow they found my blog. At this point, I was still tired of the waiting process, but I was more attentive to the things God wanted to show me.

Of course, I agreed to the engagement. I covered the radio station's Women of Wellness event in Brooklyn. It was an amazing time, and the hosts loved your girl! Toward the end of the event, they asked, "What are your plans for the future?"

"I want to write for *Teen Vogue*," I responded. Their jaws dropped. Puzzled, I just smiled, waiting for them to explain.

"Elaine Welteroth—do you know her? She'll be presenting

an award to her mentor at our awards show tomorrow night—would you like to come?"

"Know her? I *love* her. Yes, I'll come!"

I couldn't believe it.

On the train ride home, I racked my mind for what I was going to wear. It wasn't until I got home that I knew my brand-new, blush-pink jumpsuit paired with a cream tweed jacket would be exactly what I needed to meet Elaine. It screamed "boss" yet was demure. Perfect statement.

The next night, I entered the theater, found a seat near the center, and waited. I soon saw Elaine's fro enter the room, and my heart jumped. Seriously, it jumped. I'm not one who goes nuts over top influencers and celebrities, but after months of applying for random positions on the Condé Nast website, I just couldn't believe we were finally in the same room.

After the awards show, I made my way out of my row. Step by step, I began to worry if I'd be able to meet her with that large of a crowd. Dashing that fear away, I thought, *There's no way God would bring me here and I wouldn't meet her.*

And I did.

Introducing myself, I automatically began to cry. And then Elaine started to cry. It was almost as if she understood what it took for me to get there. We were hugging like crazy soon after, and when I finally was able to blink back tears, I shared how her work at *Teen Vogue* was exhilarating and exactly what the Black community, and women, needed. Periodt. Yes, the *t* is intentional.

Elaine took my phone, typed her email address in my notes, and said, "Email me." Next thing you know, she was grabbing my hand to hit the photo booth. Those lovely GIFs still exist today.

And that's how I met the former game-changing editor in chief of *Teen Vogue*.

The story doesn't end there. I needed a job, remember?

I would love to tell you that once I emailed Elaine, she answered me and I began working for *Teen Vogue*, but that's not what happened. There was still more waiting to do. Every other week, I emailed her. It was hard for me to do because I didn't want to sound annoying, but I knew she was busy, and I also knew that when the editor in chief tells you to email them, you email them.

I kept working my retail job and my website, and by then, I was working remotely for another site too. I created content for my YouTube channel and wrote my heart out. I worked, and I waited.

One day on Instagram, I came across a flyer for an awards show I was actually planning on attending. And guess who they'd just announced one of their honorees was?!

YES, girl, yes.

"Tarah-Lynn!!!" Elaine exclaimed, face-palming herself once she saw me, eyes wide. "Oh my goodness, I am so sorry. Please email me again. We'll do coffee in my office."

I emailed Elaine again but didn't hear back. The woman is busy, people! And *this* woman (i.e., me) is persistent. I couldn't relent because I knew how sincere Elaine was when she told me to reach out. I knew she meant it.

But after a few more weeks, I finally told myself, "This is it, Tarah-Lynn. This is your last time." I clicked send and went on with my day. I had sent perhaps a total of eight emails.

My phone went off ten minutes later.

It was Elaine! I responded immediately, and we planned

for my visit to her office. And then it happened, it finally happened. We met up for coffee, and though *Teen Vogue* wasn't hiring, it meant the world that she would see me.

"You are killing it," she said, looking over my résumé. "You've done all the right things. You're doing all the right things. All you have to do is wait on the right opportunity."

I was the last person who wanted to hear the word *wait* again. My face must've fallen in that moment, because that's all God was having me do!

Elaine's message was timely though. It was reassuring to know I was on the right path. It was reassuring to know I didn't have a job not because of me but simply because it wasn't time yet.

After more waiting, Elaine reached out to me to work with *Teen Vogue* on a Beautycon project. And after some more waiting, she connected me with *Teen Vogue*'s amazing fashion editor, Jessica Andrews.

Jess and I scheduled a time for me to come into the offices again for lunch. We got to know each other, and I didn't have to interview or anything. All she asked me was, "What do you want to do?"

"I want to write for *Teen Vogue*," I responded.

"Congratulations," she said, smiling.

The waiting process took over a year. That's right, over a year. Sometimes we just have to put in the work, and even then, sometimes we simply have to wait. It's not passive—*waiting* is a verb. It's an action in itself. You may not be moving, but accept that God *is*.

Patience is a virtue every monarch serving Christ needs to acquire. I think one way to develop and help you maintain this discipline is to keep in mind that when you rush God for your blessings, you cheat yourself. Keep Jeremiah 29:11 in your memory: God has a purpose and a plan for you. Indeed, you have a future in Him.

God's silence can mean a myriad of things. Sometimes He's quiet because He trusts us with a certain decision. Sometimes He's quiet because He is testing our patience. And sometimes He's quiet to see if we are really listening. God is always speaking—we just have to be in position to hear Him.

It takes time. Growth. Understanding that what we want won't come in what we consider a "timely manner." In the moments when you feel like nothing is happening, God is molding you.

So yes, you will have to wait. It will be grueling, it will hurt, and it will agitate the mess out of you—but you will see how better equipped you are to handle your blessings after the wait and toil.

Kingdom Keys

- God is moving for you in the waiting.
- We have no idea what God is saving us from and what He's saving us for.
- Our waiting period might feel like years, but it is a second that passes for God. His timing is perfect.

Reflection: *What is God telling you in the midst of your waiting?*

A PURPOSE-FILLED REIGN

The magnets on my refrigerator tell the childhood stories of my siblings and me. There's a particular one that always jumps out at me upon entering our kitchen.

It says, "I'm an accelerated reader"—a small prize I won in the first grade at Roosevelt Elementary School. Within the frame is a photo of me: my hair perfectly parted into six braids, topped off with navy-blue barrettes, my nautical-styled collar pressed to perfection by my mother the night before.

We'd wear church clothes on school picture day, my siblings and I. I quickly learned: when you carry yourself well, you can conquer the world.

I don't remember when my love for fashion began, but the photos around my house often remind me of my parents' immaculate taste in dressing my siblings and me since birth. And when I started to document my own style by taking pictures with a pink Nikon SLR camera I begged my parents to purchase, my passion was taken to new heights.

The media further encapsulated my budding passion. *Seventeen* was my favorite magazine subscription; I have a serious collection. Like typical teenagers, I would borrow my friend's *Teen Vogue* issues and she'd borrow mine, raving over who wore what.

I also watched numerous fashion shows, the first being *Kimora: Life in the Fab Lane*. Anyone used to be obsessed with Baby Phat?

I was convinced I would be a fashion designer whenever that show came on. And when I won another competition—this time in art class—it felt like a sign. I used my new sketch pads and pencils to create my own clothing collection.

However, nothing compared to my love for the early seasons of *America's Next Top Model* and then *Project Runway*. For *ANTM*, I loved the adventures, the photo shoots, the models. And of course, Tyra taught me how to "smize" (smile with your eyes)—a skill I deemed necessary for my magazine cover dreams. As for *Project Runway*, seeing the imaginative looks come together thrilled me.

These shows depicted a world I knew I was going to be in. And I thought I knew my exact position. However, I knew nothing about sewing, and I also didn't go to school for fashion. #Fail.

I was under the right umbrella, the proper house, but there was a certain seat I needed to occupy. I was taken by the hand and ushered to my seat through life experiences.

Unlike any typical Caribbean parents, mine didn't want me to be a doctor, lawyer, or nurse. My parents supported my fashion dreams but desired I do something else in the field; they wanted stability for me. They were receptive to my merging of fashion and media knowledge through the opportunities I received from starting my own brand.

I remember the moment perfectly when the digital world showed them all the possibilities one could work toward.

It was 2014 when my readers nominated *Adorned in Armor* as the Best International Fashion Blog in the Cosmopolitan UK Blog Awards. My jaw dropped when I saw my name among the finalists chosen by the editors. And when my school sponsored my trip to London, I think it was the first moment that showed me "God is up to something in this."

And He was. He *is*.

The shock never settles in that I am a business owner. That I contribute to *Teen Vogue*. That I am a fashion influencer. That I am writing this book. That I am using my passions to help people celebrate who they are.

One thing I've learned is nothing is for naught. Every moment is purposed, so we must pay close attention to where we're placed. Our passions deserve attention.

Sometimes we have to figure our passions out. Sometimes it's easy, and our passions make perfect sense, and sometimes it isn't. But when God's hand is on your life, He will never put you where you weren't supposed to be.

Think of the things your heart races for. Think of the desires you've had since childhood that you've been steered toward. There is always a trail of God's handiwork.

It's not uncommon to come across people not living up to their potential because they're living someone else's dream. At times, it's due to the issue of money. Other times, it's because of stubbornness; they won't let go of their childhood dreams. And sometimes, it's due to parents forcing their children to make that choice.

Despite those reasons, we have no business doing business where God hasn't placed us. He has put certain desires on our hearts to accomplish His purpose, which is for us to reflect the light of His salvation into this world. As His heirs, this isn't a role we can abdicate.

From birth, a royal is raised to be the person they are based on familial roles. But for you, it's different. Your purpose isn't passed down. It was gifted to you.

Though we have many passions, we are called to one purpose. *We are here to further God's kingdom on earth.*

God's Gracious Gifts to Us

God is the ultimate gift giver.

You can trust His presents because His only motive is profound love. God's relationship with humankind is built on love, and like any relationship, love is often demonstrated through giving. It's His way of spicing things up so we can experience His goodness to the fullest.

When we accept the best gift He can offer, eternal life through His Son Jesus Christ, His Holy Spirit guides us through this life. He gives us more and more of Him, the more we seek Him. And He also gives us special surprises: the gifts of the Spirit.

In 1 Corinthians 12:1, Paul tells the church of Corinthians he doesn't want them to be uninformed about these gifts. Same applies to us! We can't use the gifts we don't know we have—or rather, we can, but ineffectively. To avoid selfish motives, let us look to Scripture to see how we are to use these gifts and why.

In the Message version of Ephesians 4:4–6, Paul talks about our purpose within the family of God. He mentions how believers all have the same journey to travel so we must stay together spiritually and physically. We have one leader, one faith, one baptism, one who reigns over us all—the One who works through us all and lives in us all. Because of this, everything we are, everything we say and do is doused in the unity we find in Christ.

Though we are one, that doesn't mean we have to look, speak, and behave the same. Christ is so generous that each one of us has our own gifts (v. 7).

Christ is creative and can use His gifts in us to influence the fashion industry, music, sports—anything! The Scriptures mention (several times) how we all have gifts, each differing in types and levels, that God has lavished upon us.

People often master their talents and then use them to flourish in their careers or avocations, but our gifts from God should be utilized to make our family of believers stronger! We have to use these gifts well to serve one another (1 Pet. 4:11).

When we are faithful over what God has given us, our family is able to grow and is shielded from false teachings. We then have the God-given ability to reach people outside of church walls.

You are given your gifts to give them away. So when you operate from a place of love for people, from a place of gratitude toward God, you will find that God reveals your gifts to you before you are able to label them yourself.

Everyone has talents, but believers have spiritual gifts.

God wants our talents and spiritual gifts to be utilized for His glory and to minister to others. His gifts are catered to accomplishing His purpose, whereas talents can be utilized for secular purposes.

When we are encouraging, exhorting, speaking, singing, dancing, leading, writing, prophesying, empathizing, teaching, healing through our hands or healing through laughter—when we are doing whatever we do—we are not only helping people but also pleasing our God. We are all gifted to make a contribution, and because we don't deserve any of the gifts God has showered upon us, we must honor them even more so.

It is by His grace that we can find fulfillment for our work in His kingdom.

Putting Our Gifts to Use

What gift do you present to the queen—a woman with crowns, castles, heirlooms, and billions galore?

For her subjects, it's anything they give with their hearts.

This is often depicted through media coverage of the royals' official engagements, events, and walkabouts around the world. We see flowers, photos, books, stuffed animals, and trinkets of all kinds. I don't think I've ever seen Queen Elizabeth, Prince William and Kate, and now Prince Harry and Meghan pictured with empty hands when greeting well-wishers.

Each gift giver eagerly waits hours for the exchange of a lifetime—a present for one moment in the presence of a royal.

These gifts aren't cherished forever, however. According to the royal gift policy, these gifts don't become the private property of the royal family. They're categorized as "official gifts" and are recorded in order to keep inventory of them.

So where do the gifts go?

A gift could be kept (if it is less than $208 USD), integrated into the Royal Collection, kept in storage for about five years, loaned or donated to a good cause, or thrown away should there be no use for it.[1]

Dismayed at how wasteful the last option sounded? But why?

We do the same thing with our own gifts. Perhaps not the physical ones. But the spiritual ones definitely . . . the gifts God gave us.

Which gifts from God have you thrown away? Which ones have been dormant in the storage of your heart? Which gifts do you merely gaze upon as decoration? Which ones have you donated to every good cause except the cause of Christ?

Our royal duty is to bring praise to God through whatever He has presented to us. And yet, many believers are not operating this way.

There are many reasons why we don't use our gifts. Let's begin with the biggest culprit of them all: comparison.

I have found jealousy is paramount when we get on the conversation of gifts. And in a family of believers, that only hinders us and our mission.

How often have you heard any of these?

"She can sing, but she can't *sing* sing."

"She's only doing this for attention."

"They're paying her to do this."

"Worship team sucks."

If you have said anything along these lines, girl, you're hating!

Comparing your gift to someone else's does nothing for you and nothing for the body of Christ. No gift is worth more than another. We can all learn from one another and serve each other with what we have.

Do you feel God can't use you? Every part of your story makes for an amazing testimony.

Do you feel God hasn't given you much? Anything from Him is enough! Psalm 34:10 tells us that when we trust the Lord, we will lack no good thing.

Don't waste your gifts. Whatever you have, use it with all that you are and use it for the glory of God. The kingdom is waiting for you to unwrap it and play your part.

Kingdom Keys

- Pay attention to your placement and your passions.
- Your purpose isn't passed down; it was gifted to you.
- Though we have many passions, we are called to one purpose: furthering God's kingdom on earth.
- Don't waste your gift. Someone out there is counting on it.

Reflection: Are there any gifts you've been neglecting?

Sixteen

QUEEN OF HEARTS

Queens serve.

That probably sounds like an unusual juxtaposition of words, something completely foreign. I can totally understand why. Don't queens have servants do all the work? If I am to see myself as a royal, why must I leave my palace and head out to God knows where?

Because God is there and He's calling us there too.

The one thing believers often forget is our responsibility to serve. We get so caught up with our own lives and our own needs that we neglect those whose lives are on the line, those who need more.

How do we get to this place? Sometimes it's because of selfishness. We don't serve because we think someone else is going to do it. Or we don't serve because we simply didn't know of the need.

However, God's Word says, "The worship that God wants is this: caring for orphans or widows who need help and keeping yourself free from the world's evil influence. This is the kind of worship that God accepts as pure and good" (James 1:27 ERV).

In these verses, we see the heart of Christ. Worship is action—a call to action. We are clearly directed to the very things God finds most important: making the forgotten feel remembered and remaining set apart for His purpose.

It's not the first time the Bible mentions those less fortunate. The New Testament is filled with miracles Jesus performed for them, illustrating His avid attention and love. Jesus demonstrated how no one was better than another. Treating them equally, He would go out of His way for anyone—the sick, widows, and children, including orphans.

And when Paul went up to Jerusalem, he didn't have to follow any religious laws or customs to be accepted by the apostles because they recognized God within him. The *only* thing they required of him was that he continue aiding the poor. In Galatians 2:10, Paul says this is something he has "always been eager to do."

Like Paul, we must look after the marginalized in our society. Service is our duty—a duty we are to take on with eagerness and with a heart of compassion, empathy, and most of all love.

This duty took on a new meaning when I wore a crown. A few chapters ago, I mentioned how I traveled to Haiti to cover an event for *Teen Vogue*. Though I was there for work, I made sure I met up with my family who lives there, of course. But I also reached out to a friend, Stephanie, and her husband, Marc.

Stephanie had only recently left her home in Miami to find work in Haiti, and Marc had left his home in Philadelphia to serve as a pastor in Haiti a few weeks after they got married. He works with Tearfund Haiti, a Christian charity serving the greatest needs around the world.

A few days before my trip, I woke up with a strong urge to visit a school in Haiti. Remembering Stephanie worked at one, I asked if we could set something up so I could visit the children. I was cutting it close with it being so last-minute and considering our busy schedules. I worried it wouldn't happen, but Stephanie made it work!

Once I landed in Haiti, my aunt was there to greet me and take me to her relative's house. I quickly changed my clothes, put on my Miss Black New Jersey crown, and was on my way to Quisqueya Christian School.

Entering the school, I felt my heart would burst. The happiness I saw in the eyes of those children can't compare to anything in the world. Black and white—they rushed to hug me, hold my hand. Some were shy but eventually made their way over when they saw I had Snapchat. All were mesmerized by the crown.

And that is when I knew. I wasn't just there to serve; I realized just how much I had a heart for my people.

I visited a few classrooms with the elementary-aged students and had one final session with the teenagers. They had questions; they had stories; they had so much hope. And I was reminded of how God wants that for all His people. We are to bring hope.

When I got home, my mom was so touched by how badly I wanted to go back. She confessed her drea m to me that day: "I've always wanted to help girls in Haiti. Now, you can."

I'll be honest and say I don't have a game plan. I don't know how I will help, and I don't know when, but her words still ring in my ear: "Now, you can."

And so I say to you: you can. You can make a difference by using what you have. You can change things just by showing up. You can be a reminder to people that God's love reaches beyond what our feeble eyes can see.

I was reminded of this on the second mission trip I went on with my church. This time, I wasn't the only "youth" there; my sister, Medgina, came along too.

This mission trip was different from start to finish. God revealed to my pastor that He was leading us to Cuba, though we had no connections there. Nevertheless, my pastor obeyed. And days after, a pastor from Cuba, Pastor Jacinto, reached out to him.

Pastor Jacinto, who I now lovingly call "Grandpa," was to be the one guiding us. And let me tell you—that, he did! The eighty-three-year-old travels high mountains and low valleys to speak the Word of God. He has a vigor and a joy that cannot be contained. It's as if the Holy Spirit was a winding tornado from the top of his head to the soles of his feet.

We had to rely on the Holy Spirit to guide us every step of the way in a foreign land. Not knowing what we'd be doing until we were led taught me to wait, to pray, to listen and then watch. It trained me to focus on the mission at hand.

Since Cuba is a communist country, we had many restrictions on what we could and couldn't do. God didn't send us out into the streets this time but straight into the church. We fellowshiped, encouraged, shared resources. With countless hours on the road, we traveled all across Cuba—seven hotels in ten days.

God wanted to demonstrate to the Cuban people that He was thinking of them. They were overjoyed and often teary-eyed. One man said he felt like the world wanted Cuba off the map, so our presence in their neighborhood reminded them how much they are loved and how God has never forgotten about them.

So you see, it's not at all about you and it's not at all about me. But allow me to tell you about a time anxiety almost crippled me and had me thinking otherwise.

I actually didn't want to go on that mission trip.

The year before my Cuba trip, I enthusiastically said yes to attending my church mission trip to the Dominican Republic. Moments after agreeing to the last-minute opportunity, a Pinterest photo popped onto my iPhone screen. It reminded me that sometimes God calls us to a place far away, away from what we know, in order to truly connect with Him.

At a time when I was dealing with emotional heaviness, the trip gave me purpose. I knew God wanted me there. I came home rejuvenated and excited to continue to share God's love and resuscitating hope.

When the time came to write my name down on the list for my second mission trip, I said yes again . . . but I didn't know that assured answer would soon waver.

With gearing up to finish graduate school, juggling freelance jobs, and fulfilling my role as a pageant titleholder, I didn't have much time to think about the mission. The last few months prior to the trip were quickly upon me. I sat apprehensively at our mission trainings, wanting to say, "No, never mind."

About two months prior to leaving, I did. I told my pastor I couldn't go. I expressed how I wanted to, but my list of responsibilities was overwhelming me. In fact, merely thinking about the mission brought on scenarios in my mind of having an anxiety attack on the trip. I was just trying to get things done—my pageant would be the week following my return from the trip, after all.

I'm not an "excuses" kind of woman. My yes is my yes, and my no is my no. But anxiety had me looking at my schedule like, "Ummm, maybe not!" However, between wanting to keep my word and hearing encouraging messages from my friends and family, I ended up sticking to my yes.

In our final church service before heading off to Cuba, our missionary group sang "People's Praise" by Hector Gabriel in front of our congregation. The song tells the story of obedience, the relentless desire to tell the world the Good News of Jesus Christ and how His glory is our reward.

As we sang, "We will go," I felt like a total hypocrite because no—I didn't want to go anywhere.

I wanted to stay home. I wanted peace of mind here. I wanted the comfort of my room. I wanted to handle my business here so I could be prepared for school, for work, for my pageant.

I sat in the church service attempting to bat away tears as my chest heaved. I was already beginning to think of the ways in which I could bow out. We were to leave for Cuba the next day. The tightness in my chest began to subside only after church ended.

Again, what motivated me was encouragement by my closest friends and family. However, what had the final say was God's Word. I remembered my duty. On a grander scale of service, we are commissioned to go out into the world and show the love of Christ through evangelism and service.

God's Word says, "Therefore, go and make disciples of all the nations, baptizing them in the name of the Father and the Son and the Holy Spirit. Teach these new disciples to obey all the commands I have given you. And be sure of this: I am with you always, even to the end of the age" (Matt. 28:19–20).

Mic drop. This was the very last thing Jesus said before He ascended into heaven. Consider the importance of such a final statement. It isn't a request; it is a requirement.

We may feel like we can't serve people because we're facing our own struggles, but our obedience to God covers us. Serving God despite what's before us will make us true worshipers. We can't let the struggles we see with our natural eyes block our awareness of the supernatural.

If you're thinking you don't have the means to serve, check out your local area for how you can help. You can be faithful to God's cause right where you are. Our mission even includes family—service begins at home (1 Tim. 5:8).

> The LORD opens the eyes of the blind.
> The LORD lifts up those who are weighed down.
> The LORD loves the godly.
> The LORD protects the foreigners among us.
> He cares for the orphans and widows,
> but He frustrates the plans of the wicked.
> (Ps. 146:8–9)

If God is thinking of them, it is our duty to take society's most vulnerable seriously. We simply can't afford to disobey one of the most important commandments. Mark 12:30–31 tells us, "'And you must love the LORD your God with all your heart, all your soul, all your mind, and all your strength.' The second is equally important: 'Love your neighbor as yourself.' No other commandment is greater than these."

Get this: the Bible says if we don't love our neighbors—people we can see—and we claim we love God—whom we can't see—we're flat-out liars (1 John 4:20). You won't want to hear this, but if it is in your power to help people you can't stand to be around, do it. And don't just do it for the world to see.

In this digital age, I find we are quick to broadcast everything. It's not uncommon to come across viral videos of kind acts done by people around the world. They're heartwarming to watch, a reminder that there are people who have it in their hearts to care out loud.

And then there's the negative aspect. You can come across a post on Instagram of a video of a man in his car calling out to a homeless man to hand him cash . . . on his own camera. Yes, not caught in the act *but on his own camera*. Or the student who poses near a family on the street to take a selfie to capture how he gave them all a McDonald's Happy Meal. Or the couple who visits a third world country to serve and post on social media, only to forget about them until next year.

You can sometimes tell whether someone is acting out of their love for people or their love for praise. This false modesty is a disease. Parading our good deeds around for all to see not only exploits those in the struggle but also goes against what Jesus said.

> Watch out! Don't do your good deeds publicly, to be admired by others, for you will lose the reward from your Father in heaven.

> When you give to someone in need, don't do as the hypocrites do—blowing trumpets in the synagogues and streets to call attention to their acts of charity! I tell you the truth, they have received all the reward they will ever get. . . . Give your gifts in private, and your Father, who sees everything, will reward you. (Matt. 6:1–2, 4)

Would you rather hear, "Oh my gosh, you're such a great person" from people here on earth or "Well done" said by our King?

Tabitha, or Dorcas, chose the latter. In Acts 9:36, she is introduced to us as a disciple of Jesus—yes, a woman disciple. Stationed in the city of Joppa, Tabitha was dedicated to charitable deeds. Scholar Robin Gallaher Branch says:

> Luke's description of Tabitha makes it easy to imagine her home as welcoming, open and full of people. Luke indicates that Tabitha's home functioned as a community center for believers. . . . Quite likely her home became a drop off point for donations as she served as a reliable conduit for goods and services for believers and the wider Joppa citizenry.[1]

Particularly, Tabitha sewed beautiful garments and tunics for the needy. Writer Laurel Meyer speaks more of Tabitha's sacrifice:

> In those days, ordering and purchasing materials, cutting, assembling, fitting, altering and sewing garments, cloaks and robes by hand were tedious and labor-intensive endeavors. She willingly gave of her time and effort to help others. It takes a very emotionally, physically and spiritually strong woman to consistently and personally see to the needs of others.[2]

Tabitha was a treasure in the community, so when she fell ill and died, they were heartbroken. They quickly called for Peter when they heard he was in town. When Peter arrived, he entered the room to find it filled with women bawling their eyes out. Clutching on to their garments, they shared how her kindness had blessed them and were eager to show him the garments Tabitha had designed for them.

Peter must've been moved by the love and despair in the room because he simply sent them downstairs and began to pray. When he finished, he said, "Tabitha, get up," and sure enough, she did (v. 40 NIV).

I briefly mentioned Tabitha when I spoke of my "believe" bracelet. I explained how people will come to know Christ because of how you demonstrate His love with your own life. But allow me to add this: they will see how you serve them and will desire to serve the same God. They will speak of the goodness of God because of your demonstration.

Queens, I urge you to get up and see how you can make an impact in someone's life today. We must have a heart that mirrors Christ. When we obtain this, it makes our sacrifice of time and energy worth it. And whether your sacrifice is big or small, you will be rewarded for it. Whether it is obvious or one that only you know about, you will be rewarded for it. God sees what you put on hold to tend to His instructions. He does not overlook your obedience. Your reward is on its way.

I allowed a few weeks to go by before I unpacked my luggage from my trip to Haiti. Unzipping my suitcase, I reached for my crown. At the time, I didn't have a case for it, so I had wrapped it in bubble wrap and cushioned it between my clothing. I unraveled it carefully, eyeing the crown the same way little girls would whenever I served that year. On closer inspection, I realized two stones were missing and a corner was bent. A fleeting rush of worry came over me; my reign had only begun, and I started to beat myself up about taking my crown along on the journey without proper protection. I was instantly reminded and determined to remember that even with a damaged crown, all was worth it.

I was reminded of this again toward the end of my reign when I hosted a small pageant for elementary school girls in an urban area. Their mothers gushed about how happy they were to see a queen of color. I was reminded of the saying "representation matters," and surely, it does. But may we consider that statement not only when looking at the color of our skin; may we also remember it as we go out into the world to serve and represent Christ.

As I squatted to crown the winners that day, one of the youngest placed her hand on mine, putting her little fingers in the empty spaces. I wore that crown with those precious stones missing, but I realized I gained something way more valuable—a softened heart.

Kingdom Keys

- Be sensitive to the needs of those society casts out.
- Actions speak louder than words, but we don't have to broadcast them everywhere.

- The approval of others should never be the motivating factor for the good we do.
- There is always an area into which we can pitch a helping hand.

Reflection: *Have you become desensitized to the injustices and atrocities of this world? How can you make a difference where you are?*

Seventeen

YOU ARE SEEN

It was 1967 when the late Aretha Franklin released "Respect" onto American airwaves. Unleashing an unapologetic anthem for women's and civil rights, the Queen of Soul crossed racial borders, publicly demanding what couldn't be denied any longer: respect from man. The song shocked the masses and remained number one for no less than *twelve weeks*.[1]

Today, women are creating their own renditions of Franklin's hit. We are unapologetically spelling out R-E-S-P-E-C-T in media, movements, education, politics, and the workplace. We have discovered new ways to demand attention—women are louder than ever, and I love the sound.

Together, on a cultural and societal scale, there is progress being made in the realms of recognition. But it leads me to wonder: Where are we on a more personal level—where are we by our lonesome? Are we truly being respected, represented . . . are we being seen? From what it looks like, I would argue the answer is no. At least, not all the time.

I see a little girl's cry for attention, craving the love of her mother in a sea of other siblings. I see a teen's cry for attention, taking up drugs to escape the abuse at home. I see a woman's cry for attention through the oversharing on social media, trying to lure a love she never got elsewhere.

Can't relate? Maybe you were passed over for a job, you're feeling unappreciated in your relationships, or you're tired of raising your hand in class only to have your professor never call on you. Whatever it is, whether you've experienced this feeling once, sometimes, or always, it isn't uncommon. You aren't alone.

The moment when I remember feeling most unseen was in fifth grade. I know I'm throwing it way back, but I just have to tell you about this guy who had the biggest crush on me, and I couldn't stand him for the life of me. Let's call him James.

Where I was quiet and reserved, James was loud and boisterous. He was like a Sour Patch Kid, bullying me every chance he got and then being super sweet when he got tired of the day's cruelties. Everyone loved him, even me, when he wasn't being a jerk.

One day at choir practice, I snapped. Quiet or not, I had a mouth on me when it came to comebacks.

Shocked, James retreated to lick his wounds in private, but when he returned? Oh man, when he returned, he had it in for me. Let me tell you what he did, y'all.

He *ignored* me.

You'd think that would be a blessing, right? It could've been, if he hadn't been so obnoxious about it. He spent hours acting as if I wasn't there. Hours!

As I spoke to my friends, he would cut me off. When they would respond, he would ask them, "Who are you talking to?" To anyone entering choir practice late, he announced there was an empty seat while pointing right at me. And for the grand finale, he sat on me. Yes, he sat on me to further solidify the idea that I wasn't there. While on my lap, he turned to the right of me to speak to my best friend as if nothing was out of the norm.

Sorry, guys. I don't remember how the story ended. I have a vague sense I shoved him off as my friends yelled at him, indignant. Or maybe he saw the sadness in my eyes juxtaposed with my clenched fists. The point is even if it isn't this extreme, people will make you feel unseen. Mean girls aren't the only ones you should look out for. You can be ignored blatantly or mistakenly, but it doesn't mean it'll hurt any less.

Have you ever been asked, "If you could possess any superpower, what would it be?"

I've recently discovered I would choose the power of healing—but that's beside the point. Throughout the years, friends, strangers, and pretty much anyone answered they would want to fly or have super strength. But there is always that one person who responds they would want to be invisible.

Their reasoning is occasionally backed up by goodwill. Mostly, they express their suspicions of people and sometimes their own insecurities. I am always intrigued with this imaginary choice of power because there are so many people trying to escape invisibility as their reality.

The desire to be seen comes into play when our needs aren't being met. It doesn't always mean you feel worthless, although how you see yourself does often correlate with how you believe you are perceived by others. Whatever the cause, the real, loving power of Jesus can help you relinquish that. Even if no one else does, take solace that God sees you and wants you to own who you are.

I went to my first Hillsong Colour Conference in 2018, and it was mind-blowingly good. The theme was "Wind in Her Sails," and the team went above and beyond to make us feel as if God Himself was blowing His breath on us, propelling us forward to walk into all He is calling us to be. The production team opened the conference with a powerful demonstration of a singer on a moving boat onstage and midway through, they performed a dance routine to "This Is Me" from *The Greatest Showman*—a song about finally standing up after being ostracized by society. And when the lights went out and stars appeared above us, Hillsong artists ministered with beautiful songs from their *There Is More* album. All through the weekend, women young and old were reminded of the power of their existence, even those who were battling feeling small and insignificant.

One point I remember is when Bobbie Houston preached about the less popular women in the Bible. I remember, because it was the first time I had ever heard of Phoebe.

In Scripture, however, Paul thought highly of her:

> Now, let me introduce to you our dear and beloved sister in the faith, Phoebe, a shining minister of the church in Cenchrea. I am sending her with this letter and ask that you shower

her with your hospitality when she arrives. Embrace her with honor, as is fitting for one who belongs to the Lord and is set apart for him. I am entrusting her to you, so provide her whatever she may need, for she's been a great leader and champion for many—I know, for she's been that for even me! (Rom. 16:1–2 TPT)

That's it. Well, I'm actually being generous in providing you that lofty paragraph. Many translations are extremely condensed versions of the two verses. That may be why we've overlooked her, but it's now time to give our girl Phoebe some shine. Or at least try to.

A Zondervan study tells us:

We know nothing of this pious female who delivered Paul's "inestimable packet." . . . We just have the brief mention of her name and service. Phoebe, a devout Christian, bore without change and without reproach the name of the Moon-Goddess of the Greeks. The goddess Artemis, known by the common epithet "Phoebe," was supposed to have been identified with the light of the moon. But the Phoebe whom Paul so highly commended shone as a light for Jesus, the "Light of the World." That she must have been a woman of some consequence appears from the fact that she planned a long journey to Rome on business of her own and offered to convey to the saints there Paul's letter—"an inspired masterpiece of logic which struck the keynote of orthodoxy for the universal Church through all the succeeding ages."[2]

In fifty-some words, Paul gives us a beautiful cameo of this saintly servant of Christ for whom he urged the saints at Rome to do their utmost. The importance of her visit is indicated by the appeal of Paul to the Romans to "help her in whatever matter she may have need of."

So we don't know much about Phoebe, but we do know this: this woman was the real deal. Her name wasn't just thrown into the letter; she came first, and Paul set her apart from the rest. She was highlighted as an authoritative figure, a trusted messenger.

Phoebe was a sister in Christ, serving the one and only God we serve. She was also a leader in the church as well as a benefactor. This was huge because she was all these things *and* single.[3] For a woman to provide for herself and others and the church?! She was the emblem of excellence. It is argued Phoebe was a deaconess, but title or not, she was a force to be reckoned with. God used her to spread the Good News.

In the times of the Bible, society was patriarchal, period. Men ruled everything from their fields and homes to their wives. It's a wonder that Phoebe was able to have her own voice *and* have influential people hold her in high regard in that type of environment. Through these brief lines honoring her presence, we are able to pause and ponder what life must've been like for her. We also learn this one important fact: contrary to what the world argues, women are and have always been of great importance to God.

Christ wasn't anti-women; He was a champion for them. We are continually reminded of how He ordered care for widows. We saw how God used Esther to save a nation. Lydia, a successful business owner of a rare purple cloth product, quickly converted and didn't take no for an answer when it came to hospitality or spreading the Good News of Christ.

Rahab, a former prostitute, carried His bloodline. And when Martha was angry that she was left alone to tend to the house, Christ commended Mary for doing what mattered most: listening at His feet.

Queen, we don't have to feel confined to one house of ministry. We belong at the feet of Jesus, doing His will. Phoebe and all the other women who had little to no mention did just that.

To me, this just exemplifies we don't have to do the most to be recognized. Our society feeds on productivity and attention, but when we are in Christ, we must be comfortable in our calling. We don't have to do more when we are doing our best, especially with little.

I now see myself as an introverted extrovert. I enjoy time to myself, but I also enjoy people. I thrive on stages and in one-on-ones. I interact in group conversations as well, but it takes up a lot of my energy. At networking events, I take the initiative to approach people. I also enjoy parties—mostly because I love dressing up and simply being around friends.

But when it's time to chill, it's. time. to. chill. That quiet girl will still be a part of me; I wouldn't attempt being someone I'm not to gain attention. However, the past will try to remind you of moments when you felt forgotten. It will attempt to take you to a place where you feel as if your presence wouldn't be missed. Use these memories to push you further in knowing you are already seen by the One who matters most. Unless that's who you are, ease off the extra-ness. You can just *be*.

The letter Phoebe carried also reminds me of the power of marriage. In the next line, Paul greets Priscilla and her husband, Aquila, a ground-shaking example of how one's purpose isn't diminished after getting a man.

Your influence is tied to Christ. Your ministry doesn't end in marriage. In fact, if you're married, your marriage is a ministry. There is still work to do within the home and outside. As long as there is breath in your body, you have been made visible by the living God and exist to make Him known!

Whether you're hoping to be seen by that one special someone or simply want a "job well done," rest assured you are never overlooked by the omnipresent God. From the cross to overcoming the grave, Christ performed the greatest disappearing act of all time for you to come into existence.

So yes, your presence is a gift. And no, you aren't forgotten; your Father sees you. If no one understands you, understand that He does. God is "acquainted with *all* of [our] ways" (Ps. 139:3 ESV, emphasis added).

God knows and calls you by name. And if this world tries to topple you with the illusion of your voice being on mute, the reality is God hears you in heaven. If even the smallest women in the Bible have played the greatest roles, imagine the significance of your role, today, as a kingdom woman of God. Phoebe barely had a proper paragraph in the Bible, but that didn't take away from her power. Don't let the feeling of being unnoticed take away yours.

When the Queen of Soul sat down to record "Respect," it was Valentine's Day. I find it ironic that a top hit with the theme of demanding attention was recorded on a day of the year when women can feel so alone.

The anthem gave women a voice to stand for what they deserve. And so I say to you, you deserve the same thing.

You are demanding attention when you believe you are seen, heard, and valued by God. Stop waiting on someone to see you so you can finally see yourself. God will always say, "I choose you."

It's time to choose yourself.

Kingdom Keys

- God sees you even if others don't.
- Women are of great importance to God; He champions us.
- God takes our past and transforms us into the women He intended us to be for the present.
- There is power in your presence.

Reflection: *What titles were you given that you didn't want?*

Eighteen

TREASURE

Sis, God may hide *you* in plain sight.

Have you ever wondered why your girls are getting married and you can't seem to find a single prospect? It seems everyone is living happily ever after with their princes and you're left sitting in the pumpkin. You don't feel like treasure anymore; you've begun to believe no man will step forward to ask you to dance.

And so you take things into your own hands. Even scouring places where you know a *true* prince isn't going to be. Thing is, you've got the quest backward. The answer has always been right in front of your face.

This isn't your mission.

I know, I know. Dating is different these days. One can initiate conversation on Facebook through clicking "like." On Instagram, it goes down in the DMs. And on Tinder, simply swipe right.

Like everything else, there's a good and a bad side when it comes to these dating apps. Most of the time, the men you match with are looking for short-term physical relationships. They don't want to be committed. On the other end, social media opens a whole new world of possibilities, occasionally bringing about the perfect matches. I personally know mature believers who have met online and are happily married. So that's not out of the question.

Dating has always been glorified. The chase, the world says, is fun. We see it in fairy tales, we see it in media, we see it in church and in our own circles. The questions come flying, and everyone suddenly is tuned in to watching your love life like reality television. Getting a new man seems to always make headlines.

I know you feel it: the pressure to settle or run after any man who tries to saunter his way into your DMs. But you aren't a conquest. If you desire something true and lasting, I encourage you to wait. And if you feel you've been waiting enough, wait some more.

There is absolutely nothing wrong with you. You are a queen, and the proper suitor will pursue you. You're worth the search and you're worth fighting for.

Worthy

Bruno Mars's "Treasure" crooned through my car speakers as I drove down the highway. The man is a master lyricist. He's so smooth with it, always choosing the perfect words to make a woman feel she is the only one he sees. As I sang the last line of the chorus, I smiled as I reflected on his request. Chivalry isn't dead, y'all—he was *asking* the woman if she would allow him to treat her the way she deserved to be treated.

The sweet song led me to focus on one thing. Whether a man asks or whether he demands, not every man *deserves* to treasure you.

As women of the kingdom, we are royalty even without a prince. We are to set standards for whom we choose to rule alongside us. And no, this is not about being picky. You're not acting like you're "too good"—you simply know your worth. No matter what family or friends say about your taste, trust and believe there's nothing wrong with the right expectations.

Sometimes it is easy to go off course and settle because you feel all the "good guys" are gone. As you continue to seek Christ, you won't want to settle and will recognize what aspects of yourself you want a man to complement and encourage.

One thing God doesn't want is an unequally yoked relationship. The Message version of 2 Corinthians 6:14 tells us, "Don't become partners with those who reject God."

When Christ is seated on the throne of your heart, you cannot go into covenant with someone who will defile His temple. Or a lukewarm man who doesn't know the power of Jesus. Just because he has "God 1st" in his bio doesn't mean he's for you. If he topped it off with the prayer hand emoji—that doesn't mean he's for you. Just because he prays and goes to church doesn't mean he's a Christian. You will know by his fruit. How did he approach you? What does he post? What is his character like? Sure, he may be cute, but does he reflect Christ?

Oh, and if you want to give him a chance because he seems like a "nice guy" and you see the good in him, *please* don't. You can't change him, and you can't save him. One of the most common forms of heartbreak I see our sisters experience is when they believe otherwise. I've seen men attempt to keep up with our sisters who are so in love with Christ, and so they go to church because of her. They read their Bibles because of her. They pray because of her. And that may seem inspirational, but it's not if you (and not Christ) are his motivation for these things. If he doesn't want God for himself, you've become his god.

And then I see our sisters doing all in their power to have their men serve the Lord. They beg God, pray to God, fast for God, and God is looking down like, "I did not tell you to pursue this man." He tells us in His Word to flee from partnerships where He is nowhere involved!

It's a pointless fight. God didn't place us here to drag the boy to church. Plant the seed, and then leave. Or you will soon find yourself miserable and heartbroken over a man you lost twice: from your heart and from heaven.

To avoid it all, sis, never stray from the example of Christ. We must have that nonnegotiable set in place. If you desire an effective reign, your man must be a man of God. God's grace will cover you both. So no, your prince won't be perfect, but he'll be perfect for you.

No matter your age, create a list of everything you want your man to be. Think of everything! And I mean, everythang.

If you're hesitant because you have made mistakes in the past, make the list based off of everything your ex was *not*! Your relationships weren't a waste of time—God will use even the ugly parts of your story for His glory. Regardless of your past or current circumstances and choices, you still deserve a true prince.

As you begin to write your list or to use one you have already, you'll find that it is quite easy to think of the physical traits. And let me tell you, there is nothing wrong with wanting to be attracted to your husband, girl. Nothing whatsoever.

But let's dig into the gold mine of it all.

The best way to get started is by studying 1 Corinthians 13:4–7.

Add to your list that you want your man to be patient, kind, confident, humble, and respectful. Write that you want a man who isn't willing to compromise with the world, who isn't easily angered, and who doesn't tally all your wrongdoings against him. Write that you want a man who is honest and just, one who will never give up on you, one who will never give up on God. The one who has high hopes for your future and is in it for the long run.

If you're already in a relationship, a quick test to see whether your boyfriend or fiancé is who you should be spending your time, let alone your life, with is to read 1 Corinthians 13:4–7 again and try replacing the word *love* with his name. Pay attention to how that made you feel. Pay attention to whether it even sounded right.

If marriage is in God's plan for you, God will reveal to you the one He has set apart for you when it is time. But for now, begin to pray for his preparation. Even if you have no idea who this man will be, pray for who God will make him to be.

I'm not saying your prince will be all these things you listed. God can wrap him up perfectly for you, but sometimes He will surprise you with one you never knew you needed.

The Pursuit

For John Piper, it's not about where or how you meet a future spouse. He says, "The great question is: Are you mature enough to discern a worthy spouse?"[1]

Isn't that good? The search is less about if and when a future husband first lays eyes on you and more about who he discovers you to be. Who will he find when he sees you? And will you be spiritually equipped to realize when the perfect choice is in front of you?

I don't want you to be the woman more caught up in looking ready to be discovered than actually being prepared. This is the time to draw nearer to God and accomplish everything He sets on your heart. Time is fleeting, and the chance to know your true self is worth the process. I imagine life to be so much more beautiful when your prince has the honor of peeling back the layers of who you are.

Find out what makes you happy. Travel, take yourself out on dates. Fall in love with *you*. Stop awaiting a knight in shining armor to relieve you from your despair. You don't have to be lonely when you learn how to enjoy your own company.

I know what you're thinking: *If I'm so focused on what I can do for the kingdom, where might my future husband find me?*

When it's time, he will find you hidden in God. There's this quote I see everywhere that I always think of. Someone once said, "A woman's heart should be so close to God that a man should have to chase Him to find her." Indeed, the man worthy of your cause should be able to dig deeper.

In the medieval times, when a suitor was found for a young maiden, her father would have to pay her dowry to complete the marriage. Typically, that would consist of jewels, land, and/or animals and would set the couple up to live comfortably. The husband, however, was the one who owned it all.

We clearly don't do that today. But for the sake of this chapter, consider yourself your own dowry. Your heart contains all the riches your prince will be honored to discover.

You'll know when you've both struck gold. And you will only know when you have become so secure in your identity in Christ, fulfilling the mission God has for you in your singleness. We all have a separate calling outside of a potential future husband! This truth should be a relief.

Often women get so caught up in their desire to be boo'd up that they miss out on life. But you don't live for a man! You live for Christ, and your mate is just a bonus, should you even desire one at all.

Yes, I haven't forgotten you, ladies, who have no desire to get married or don't end up with a mate after all. As God's creations, our first call is to Him, but for some of us, God may be our entire call. As in, God alone is our purpose. "For your Maker is your bridegroom, his name, God-of-the-Angel-Armies! Your Redeemer is The Holy of Israel, known as God of the whole earth" (Isa. 54:5 MSG).

I'll never forget the day I went to a singles' conference in Brooklyn. I'll never forget it because it was a long trek my heels were not ready for. But also because of one woman in particular.

It was Q&A time, and someone asked, "As I wait, how can I be satisfied with God?"

A couple people answered along the lines of, "If God isn't enough for you, no man will ever be."

And that's totally true. We say we want a man to make us feel whole, and when we get the blessing, we soon find we still aren't satisfied. After making this discovery, we begin to put unnecessary pressures on our men when it was never their role to make us whole. Your man's only job is to love you like Christ loves the church.

It is Christ alone who brings completeness.

Another young woman was a testament of that. Grabbing the microphone, she stood up from her seat directly behind me and her voice boomed. She boldly stated that she is happy to live single for the rest of her life because of the overwhelming joy she has by being in His presence every day.

Whoa.

I felt the power in her words. Truthfully, I'm not there yet. But I truly do desire God to be enough for me.

I pray this for you too. In fact, I'll add this on my own list. May we *all* become so content with Christ that we are in constant pursuit of His love and His love alone.

Kingdom Keys

- You are worth the search—if it's in God's plan for you, your prince will find you.
- Do not settle out of impatience or pressure.
- God isn't pleased with unequally yoked relationships.
- Use discernment to know if a man is serving God and if his intentions are honest.

- Your singleness is the best time to discover yourself and who you are called to be.
- Christ is the only one who can complete us.

Reflection: How can you begin to treat yourself as treasure?

Nineteen

DRESSED FOR BATTLE

"What is the most important thing our society needs?" Stan, the pageant host, asked. I was watching *Miss Congeniality*—a movie in which Gracie, an FBI agent played by Sandra Bullock, is forced to go undercover as Miss New Jersey to prevent a terrorist attack at the Miss United States pageant.

Every contestant ahead of Gracie answered, "World peace." But when her turn came along, she was pleased to respond with a cause close to her heart.

"That would be harsher punishment for parole violators, Stan," she said, grinning from ear to ear.

His mouth agape, he turned to the now-silent audience. The camera followed his gaze, crickets chirping as the screen showed an equally displeased and uninterested crowd. Gracie, recognizing the confusion on their faces, bowed to their silence. She finished off with the stereotypical answer: "And . . . world peace."

The crowd erupted with applause.

Though I knew nothing of pageants at the time I first watched the movie, it wasn't difficult to understand the joke they were making. Answering "world peace" was the fluffiest one could get. It was the crowd-pleasing answer that further fed the belief that pageant girls were fake. It was safe. To say you stood for anything different would cause disfavor.

This hilarious scene is merely satire; I can attest to that, as one who competes. Depending on the pageant system, we're encouraged to have our own platforms. Mine has been #TarahTakesHeart, a campaign to honor my mom by raising Heart Awareness and through showing women how to treasure ourselves and take care of the very vessel that keeps us going.

I toured my home state of New Jersey, across the United States, and even abroad, dedicated not only to talking about the physical ailments that plague the hearts of women but also to covering all of the emotional, the psychological, and of course, the spiritual. I won the Heart Champion Award at nationals and still continue to work on these issues through my brand, Adorned in Armor.

You may claim your crown because of how pretty it looks, but a fight is required to carry it. It takes training, exhausting your own resources, and the courage to not back down. It takes a passion for what you stand for, dedication to a cause bigger than you.

Gracie actually stood for something, but to advance, she put aside her own beliefs for popular opinion. She was allowed this for the sake of a movie, but our own lives aren't scripted.

We are warriors of the kingdom, and our platform is Christ. So the reality is we have been recruited to fight in the Lord's battle, and backing away from our cause is detrimental. You may not see the battle with your own eyes, but you will experience it spiritually. Fluff and talk of "world peace" won't help us. In Matthew 10:34, our Commander in Chief tells us, "Don't imagine that I came to bring peace to the earth! I came not to bring peace, but a sword."

If Christ is the Prince of Peace—if He's supposedly so heavenly and kind—why does He want to wreak havoc? Why is He showing up with guns blazing?

It's not what it looks like. As believers in a war-torn, dangerous world, we commonly believe that Christ will be the one to bring an end to our discord. And He will, but not in the way you think.

In John 14:27, He leaves a gift of peace—"a gift the world cannot give." Harmonious living doesn't necessarily mirror the type of peace He will bring. I like how one writer puts it:

> The Hebrew word for "peace," shalom, is often used in reference to an appearance of calm and tranquility of individuals, groups, and nations. The Greek word *eirene* means "unity and accord"; Paul uses *eirene* to describe the objective of the New Testament church. But the deeper, more foundational meaning of peace is "the spiritual harmony brought about by an individual's restoration with God."[1]

There will be peace one day, but only after the war has ended. This war began with Lucifer, God's highest-ranking angel who rallied up his own troops to dethrone God and failed. Now kicked out of heaven, Lucifer and his fallen angels relentlessly pursue our defeat.

He began by getting us caught up in his mess through the temptation and fall of Adam and Eve, turning man against God. But Christ, the Prince of Peace, was sent to us so that we may accept Him and be welcomed into His army for the biggest fight of our lives. A fight worth fighting.

This is a spiritual battle, one that puts God's people and God's angel armies on one side and Satan and his demons on the other. Paul gives us proof of this in Ephesians 6:10–12. The God's Word translation says:

> Receive your power from the Lord and from his mighty strength. Put on all the armor that God supplies. In this way you can take a stand against the devil's strategies. This is not a wrestling match against a human opponent. We are wrestling with rulers, authorities, the powers who govern this world of darkness, and spiritual forces that control evil in the heavenly world.

Your enemies on earth are the least of your worries. In fact, they aren't your *real* enemies. We are opposed by forces we cannot see. And though we have already won the war, that doesn't mean we won't have to go off into battle. In Ephesians 6:13–18, Paul preps us with the weapons of triumph.

All this talk of fighting and war may frighten you, but Matthew 10:28 comforts us, telling us not to be afraid of those who want to kill our bodies. Why? Because they cannot touch our souls! Even when you feel like the struggles of life are closing in on you, keep victory in mind. "We are hard pressed on every side, but not crushed; perplexed, but not in despair; persecuted, but not abandoned; struck down, but not destroyed" (2 Cor. 4:8–9 NIV).

God tells us not to fear a zillion times in the Bible; He doesn't want our thoughts to be consumed by it. He has been communicating this to His people since the Old Testament. He encourages us to be strong and courageous. He promised He will never leave or forsake us (Deut. 31:6). How comforting it is to know we have the One who will go before us. How comforting it is to know we have power over good and evil.

Fight past the fear! This waging war is necessary and should not be neglected. Throughout history, you will find that even royals went off to war. As God's heirs, we must armor up and get dressed for battle too. We must equip ourselves with the Word while our King wins every victory.

We may think that when we saunter behind, we're avoiding harm. But really we are neglecting responsibility and opening ourselves to invasion of sin. With our brothers and sisters fighting at the forefront, we're left behind, more susceptible to sin.

King David fell victim to this. Yes, even the man known to be after God's heart, was the cause of his own defeat at one point. In the eleventh chapter of 2 Samuel, we learn kings typically go to war in the spring, and yet David sent the Israelite army to go on without him. Instead, he rested and decided to take in the sights from his balcony.

Right outside, he found a beautiful woman bathing, decided he wanted her, and took her to his bed. Fast-forward: she gets pregnant, he has her husband killed, and a prophet exposes what he did. There's so much more to the story, but here's my point: David would've been protected, but he put himself in that predicament when he neglected his duty in war.

"David knew he was a king but chose to ignore his true identity and stay home," author Havilah Cunnington explains. "In that moment, David forgot who he was. . . . He forgot he was made for battle. His choice to ignore his true identity left him vulnerable. . . . The moment David chose to forgo the battle was the moment David chose the balcony."[2]

Needless to say, King David faced some pretty dark times after that. Read the book of Psalms to see just how much! He fell into his own trap, yes. But he didn't pity himself; he repented and praised the God who had always won his battles.

In this life, you will have to stand for Christ. And in fighting, you will learn the battle isn't yours; it's the Lord's. So don't bow to the expectations of the world; don't allow fears, laziness, ignorance, or indifference to reign over you. Royals go off to battle too.

God will put a stop to evil once and for all. Will He find you hiding and defenseless? Or will you be at the front lines of the winning side?

Kingdom Keys

- God is fighting for us.
- There is a spiritual war going on regardless of whether we're willing to fight or not.
- We don't have to be afraid of the enemy. Satan isn't stronger than our God.

Reflection: *Not feeling strong enough? Sis, you already have the victory! I'm dedicated to equipping you with the right weapons* *on my podcast,* Dressed for Battle. *I interview warrior women of faith, and we discuss not just what we've conquered but also what we're struggling with. Join us on your favorite podcast platform and share your prayer requests @dressedforbattle podcast.*

Twenty

DEFENDING HONOR

The doorbell rang.

"Who is it?" my sister called out from the kitchen.

No one answered.

She shrugged, continuing to wash dishes as she watched an Asian rom-com on Netflix. I was eating at the table.

Moments later, my brother walked in with a small package.

"Who's it for?" I asked.

"You, duh," he said, plopping the package in the corner of the house where I kept all my other mail.

Big boxes, small boxes, and in between just waiting to be opened. Being an influencer has its perks. I often get surprise mail that I allow to pile up until I'm ready to grab my box cutter and get to work.

My mother, sisters, and I enjoy opening them together. It's our special moment to revel in new beauty products and clothing and split all the amazing goods among our small group. This time we decided to open the most recent package first.

I opened it up to see a beautiful eyeshadow palette encrusted with little rhinestones that looked like stars. They twinkled as we oohed and aahed over them.

We were enthralled with all the bold colors, envisioning looks we would create. We chattered excitedly until I noticed the palette was in the shape of a Ouija board, a tool used to communicate with the dead.

"Hex?" My sister squinted as she peered closer to read the eye color shade that popped out the most. "Isn't that like . . . related to witchcraft?"

"Uh oh!" My mother gasped. These kinds of things are especially not toyed with when you come from the Caribbean.

At times, I receive products that don't suit my family, and so I pass them along to friends, but this had to be thrown out.

And so that is what we did. We didn't leave it inside our house; we took it right outside and dumped it into our trash can.

You may think we were being dramatic and that it wasn't a big deal. But we simply do not play when it comes to our God.

The world has many things that will entice and invite us in, but that doesn't mean we should enter. It will offer us things, but that doesn't mean we should accept them. It doesn't matter how beautifully wrapped something is—if it isn't of God, it isn't for you.

When you want to serve God, you devote your very being to honoring Him in the way you live. You learn what holiness looks like, so you don't compromise with dead things. You'll grow uncomfortable being in places you have no business being. You'll refuse to get caught up in stuff just because it's a trend. You'll develop a mindset of "It looks good and feels good, but is it good for my spirit?"

This applies to the little and the big.

I've had to refuse only a couple of gifts, but there are plenty of times when I have had to turn down opportunities, whether it be press parties celebrating goddesses or Christian events that weren't really about our God. I've had moments when gigs passed me by simply because I wouldn't subscribe to the ideals of other influencers. I remained true to my faith, and I understand sometimes that means being shunned for being set apart.

Jesus was speaking about us when He said in John 17:14–15, 17–19:

> I have given them your word. And the world hates them because they do not belong to the world, just as I do not belong to the world. I'm not asking you to take them out . . . but to keep them safe from the evil one. . . . Make them holy by your truth; teach them your word, which is truth. Just as you sent me into the world, I am sending them into the world. And I give myself as a holy sacrifice for them so they can be made holy by your truth.

The English Standard Version says, "For their sake I consecrate myself, that they also may be sanctified in truth" (v. 19). We'll get to the consecration part later!

Believers often mention this passage to reference the popular phrase "In it, not of it." This phrase is used to defend how we aren't supposed to be influenced by the world, which is true. However, Jesus isn't telling us to hide in a box until He comes.

We are called to be set apart, but we aren't called to disassociate from everything. Jesus sent us out into our temporary homes on a mission: we're called to be influencers.

It's important we do our part, because Satan sure is doing his. He's keen on entrapping believers; he's extremely cunning, making his devices even appear like something God Himself would be pleased with.

At times, you may find it hard to decipher what is Christlike and what is worldly. There are so many blurred lines! However, the Bible makes it clear that Satan is the god of this world, that this world is under his influence whether the inhabitants know of it or not. He relentlessly attacks and is a snare to anyone who is trying to live a life of righteousness (Eph. 6:12).

The Bible refers to Satan as an "angel of light" (2 Cor. 11:14). He is the master manipulator, imitator, and liar. When Satan tempted Jesus, he mixed his deception with Scripture, and though he couldn't make Christ fall for it, he easily influences this world and warps the way we should live, making it seem as if cursing God's name and making a joke out of Christianity don't matter.

What do we do? Christians are instructed to be separated from the evils of this world so God can receive us (2 Cor. 6:17).

We are palace dwellers, and it is our job to invite everyone into the kingdom of God as well. Jesus broke bread with criminals, the most hated and poorest of society (Mark 2:16), but His relationship with them was not solely social; it saved them.

Therefore, it is possible—being in the world and not of it, I mean. The late Billy Graham said, "We come in contact with the world, and yet we retain our distinctive kingdom character and refuse to let the world press us into its mold."[1]

While we are here, we aren't to show contempt but a Christ-like love. We are to help the world, pray for the world, and witness to the world. And through this process, we are not to be conformed to the world.

The Bible draws the line. Its teachings make it clear that you're either black or white. There's no gray—no room for lukewarmness in the kingdom of God. Christianity is not about dos and don'ts; it's not a list of restrictions. Though the world would rather we believe that following Christ is boring, a kill-joy, and not even necessary, our faith provides us freedom to live our lives abundantly (John 10:10).

Therefore, the argument isn't what's good and what's bad; it's what's holy and what's not. What is pleasing to God and what is not.

Many people say "Christians are fake" because they're right. The ones they have met and experienced are judgmental or hypocritical. The reason Christians generally get such a bad rap is because the ones who are not living for God are in the world. To be a Christian means we are followers of Christ. We aren't Sunday Christians; we're not Easter or Christmas Christians.

We cannot call ourselves followers of Christ if all we do is pick the parts of the Bible we'll abide by. We cannot hide behind the excuse "God knows my heart," because our true hearts will be revealed through our actions. We cannot dismiss how God wants us to carry ourselves for the sake of comfort in a raging war.

It's all or nothing.

Knowing what you know now, whose side are you on? Whose name do you bear when people see you every day?

In the Bible, Paul says, "We are more than conquerors through him who loved us" (Rom. 8:37 NIV). So if you're on the winning team, the only way to overcome isn't by your own efforts. We have already won because of Jesus's sacrifice, and we continue to win lost souls by telling the world our testimony (Rev. 12:11).

In the Sermon on the Mount, Jesus explained the only way we can have true influence in every sector of the world. When we use our voices to defend our faith, we become "salt and light." Matthew 5:13–16 says:

> You are the salt of the earth. But what good is salt if it has lost its flavor? Can you make it salty again? It will be thrown out and trampled underfoot as worthless.
>
> You are the light of the world—like a city on a hilltop that cannot be hidden. No one lights a lamp and then puts it under a basket. Instead, a lamp is placed on a stand, where it gives light to everyone in the house. In the same way, let your good deeds shine out for all to see, so that everyone will praise your heavenly Father.

In the case of Christ, being salty isn't a negative thing! We are purposed to change the natural flavor of this earth by being the spiritual spice the world needs. We aren't meant to be hidden. Shine your light for the world to see, even if you risk being shunned.

Sometimes being set apart means missing out. On potential connections, potential opportunities, potential invitations.

However, it also means blessings will fall over you. It means God will honor you. He will give you a standing ovation.

The Bible tells the story of the first ever Christian martyr, Stephen. His light shined so bright that everyone took notice, including the opposition. He was bold with speaking the truth and unashamed in showing the world who he stood for. No one could find real fault with him, so a group of Jews decided to falsely accuse him.

In Stephen's final hours, God gave him power to expose Israel's rejection of their one and only Savior. He pointed out how though they were chosen, they failed when they chose the wrong team: man-made religion over relationship with Christ.

They stoned him.

Stephen kept his eyes on heaven, and before he took his last breath, he excitedly shared, "Look, I see the heavens opened and the Son of Man standing in the place of honor at God's right hand!" (Acts 7:56).

His dedication to stand firmly on the winning team of Christ still inspires believers today to defend the name of our God, regardless of the consequences. I mean, come on—the King of all kings Himself got up to His feet to welcome him into eternity!

On this earth, we may be shunned and we may even be stoned, but our Father in heaven assures us we will always be seen.

He is ready and willing to honor you, but first, defend His cause.

Your brand isn't just about you; it's about how you represent God. As an influencer for Christ, you need to represent Him well. We are the light of the world, a city on a hill, and the salt of the earth. It's time to intentionally be set apart.

"Chivalry is dead."

You've heard that said before, haven't you? I don't necessarily agree with this statement, as I've come across men who exemplify chivalry. Though the term commonly refers to how men should treat women, that's not what it solely means. And so I'd like to give some background on a time when this quality thrived.

The Middle Ages.

Merriam-Webster defines *chivalry* as "the system of values (such as loyalty and honor) that knights in the Middle Ages were expected to follow."[2] There were three types of knightly chivalry.[3] Knights had duties to countrymen, to women, and to God. They were expected to guard the poor and put the lives of others before theirs. They were gracious toward all women and loyal to one. (*Hello*, Sir Lancelot.)

As for honoring God, the knight's duty involved being devoted to God and the church, advocating for good against evil, and worshiping God above earthly rulers.

Their conduct isn't too far off from our duties as heirs of the kingdom. However, our own system of values can only be carried through when we *first* consecrate ourselves. Pastor Matthew Stevenson defines *consecration* as "pulling away from, to cling to."[4] It's ridding ourselves of worldly influence and holding on to the light of Christ.

We must pull away from this world and cling to Jesus because the human soul is always looking for someone or something to whom it can pledge allegiance. And if we're not worshiping God, guess who we're serving? Yup, you got that right. Satan.

Like chivalry, consecration is a lost art, but it is vital to a believer's life. Consecration has two objectives: to transform and to empower. When you truly experience God, you will not be the same person. The change in you occurs because He wants to empower you with a duty. Your duty is God's assignment for you.

Contrary to knights being appointed, God can call us before we even believe we have a fighting chance. But sometimes we aren't given any form of assignment, responsibility, or duty until we are first transformed.

Due to living in a fallen world, people often struggle with rejection. Therefore, being given a duty is appealing because we begin to find meaning in it. However, we're only disqualifying ourselves and sacrificing power when we choose to get to work before the transformation of our souls.

When we commit to the transformational process, our duty becomes second nature to us because it is God's grace and anointing that accomplishes our mission.

When we consecrate ourselves unto the Lord, we develop holiness. You don't get through by avoiding sin, nor is it a matter of obeying rules. Holiness comes when you spend time in the presence of the Lord. This can be done through fasting, repentance, and sanctification, which is setting yourself apart so God can work through you.

If you think you're too young to devote your life to God, consider the advice of Solomon, the wisest king to have ever lived. After a life of having it all—the women and all the finest things in life—he had an epiphany: "I observed everything going on under the sun, and really, it is all meaningless—like chasing the wind" (Eccles. 1:14). For us, there is no future outside of Christ. When we choose the world, we've seen all we needed to see.

However, in consecrating yourself, God gives you newness; He gives you meaning. He gives you vigor and surprises every day of your life when you commit to Him.

In Jeremiah 1:5, God says, "Before you were born, I set you apart and appointed you as my prophet to the nations."

You are living a life that is fulfilled in consecration because you were born for this. This process will equip you to rely on God and not on your own power. It will open your eyes to God's truth. It will open your ears to God's voice. It will honor God.

It doesn't matter how close we think we are to God, we all need a soul check. We all need to reconsecrate ourselves. "If you think you are standing strong, be careful not to fall" (1 Cor. 10:12). It's easy to get distracted by this world, but when we keep our eyes on Jesus, our feet are steady. With the help of the Holy Spirit, we honor our God when we are on our knees.

I love how Pastor Matthew Stevenson says it: "Consecration is God on the throne, you on the altar. It brings you back to the place to remind you He runs your life and not anything else you put in His place of worship."[5]

May we go back to a heart of worship. May we live our lives realizing it's all about Jesus. May we stop awaiting our knight in shining armor and take things into our own hands.

We are not damsels in distress but warrior women defending God's honor. We are women God is calling out to draw closer so that the world will see Him in us.

Kingdom Keys

- While there are so many things seeking to influence us, we are influencers by living up to God's standard.
- We are the light of the world, a city on a hill, and the salt of the earth. It's time to intentionally be set apart.
- We have to consecrate ourselves, placing God on the throne and us on the altar.

Reflection: *You are a woman of influence! In what areas can you better represent God?*

Twenty-One

CORONATION DAY

The Invitation

Let's make this official, shall we?

I'm confident you are more than ready to conquer life as the royal you are. But first, let's celebrate the preparation of your reign.

To properly symbolize and initiate one's reign, there must be a coronation. Traditionally, this occurs months after the predecessor is properly mourned. The coronation is where the sovereign is bestowed with a crown and is presented pieces of regalia, further establishing their regal power. This ceremony forever marks not only the nation but also world history.

The process is actually quite intricate and extensive. In 1953, Queen Elizabeth II's coronation service took three whole hours! It fell into six portions: "the recognition, the oath, the anointing, the investiture (which includes the crowning), the enthronement and the homage."[1]

The vow Queen Elizabeth had to take has transformed over the centuries, and today, the royal must swear to reign in accordance to law, to be just and merciful—represented by the four swords in the Crown Jewels—and to uphold the Church of England. Talk about responsibility.

The monarch then sits in the late, late, late, late . . . King Edward's chair, a throne built in 1300 and passed down to every royal since 1626. That is where Elizabeth was "anointed, blessed and consecrated" by the Archbishop of Canterbury, the supreme governor and highest cleric of the Church of England.[2]

The orb and scepters, the monarchy's most authoritative symbols of God's power and the monarch's temporal power, were then presented to her. After Queen Elizabeth II received them, St Edward's Crown, made of solid gold, was placed on her head. She also got a fancy robe, bejeweled sword, ring, and other emblems of English monarchy.

Finally, homage is paid to the sovereign and Holy Communion is celebrated. Most recently, it has become tradition for the royal family to present themselves on the Buckingham Palace balcony prior to going to the coronation banquet there.

For Queen Elizabeth II's coronation, invitations were sent to clergy, nobles, government officials, special guests, and representatives of other countries. Even the young Prince Charles received his own special invitation—kid-styled, of course. In total, Elizabeth's coronation ceremony had an attendee list of 8,251 guests, with 129 nations represented. It was a lavish affair.

While it would be an honor to get an invite to the next coronation—and oh, how amazing it would have been to have attended Prince Harry and Meghan Markle's fairy tale of a wedding—we have the greatest celebraton of all time to prepare for.

Jesus talks about our invitation to His Great Feast in Matthew 22:2–14. He paints the picture of heaven's kingdom. And I just *love* that He compares the kingdom of God to a party.

We often think church life is stuffy and boring, but He's demonstrating that His Father's business is anything but. He wants us to enjoy Him, to laugh freely and feast. Quite frankly, God wants us to turn it up for Jesus! And He wants us to invite our friends, family, and whoever we come across with that same excitement.

God invited the Jews into His kingdom, but many checked off "no" when Jesus approached them with the message: "Repent [change your inner self—your old way of thinking, regret past sins, live your life in a way that proves repentance; seek God's purpose for your life], for the kingdom of heaven is at hand" (Matt. 4:17 AMP).

Jesus approached His own people, and still, many denied the King's Son (John 1:11). They had every reason to accept Him, but instead, they gave flimsy excuses for skipping the banquet.

God was rightfully enraged and said they would never taste the feast. I mean, it wasn't the first time the guests had heard of the wedding. It's not like they could FedEx in those times—when preparing an event, the host would have to send an initial message to make them aware there was something going on. And then they would have to travel out in the streets again to let them know the feast was prepared. They had their chance.

So you see, even if you decline, Jesus will ask for you to come again and again. But there will come a day when God will deem it too late for you to come (Matt. 22:8). Like the parable demonstrates, it is up to you to choose.

In response to those who said no, God basically was like, "Forget the guest list; let's focus on inviting everyone else."

And so the very invitations that went out to the elite went out to everyone else as well. This is integral to note because it grouped together all people, including those the Pharisees (like today's society) considered to be at the bottom of the barrel. Jesus invited those who were ill, those who were poor, tax collectors, prostitutes, and other sinners to join in on the celebration.

God has promised to love those who are not loved and to invite everyone into the land of the living (Hosea 2:23). The offer of salvation, a symbol of God's grace, is extended to all, "to the ends of the earth" (Acts 1:8).

Indeed, God will go to great lengths so everyone gets the invitation. He loves you so much He wants a kingdom filled with you, your family and friends, and the very people you think shouldn't be invited. He wants you as a guest of honor at the banquet table; He wants the table to be full of smiling, expectant faces.

But you can't enter in just any old way.

It's a mighty privilege to be asked to come to the party of eternity. While everyone is invited and everyone is pursued time and time again, God expects us to come correctly.

Are you thinking, *Whatever happened to come as you are?* That still stands. The point God is making is that you can enter in *only* through His Son, Jesus.

The parable mentions God noticed a guest who was not wearing the wedding robe that was *provided* for him. When

God asked him why he wasn't dressed, the man had no words. He chose to try to gain entry on his own terms.

This guy messed it up on his own and, of course, was thrown out. How do you come to a party not dressed to party?! It's disrespectful to the host, especially when He has provided you the very items you need to come prepared. You will find yourself dressed for the ball when you believe in the death and resurrection of Jesus and accept the gift of the Holy Spirit.

Remember, you are no commoner. You have been given a royal invitation into the kingdom of God when you accept and celebrate His Son, Jesus, through the life you live.

Will you RSVP yes to the invitation?

Will you say yes to reconciliation with God?

Yes to Christ?

Yes to the crown?

Or will you be like those who rejected the invite, deciding that a relationship with the King was at the bottom of their priorities?

Crowned

Contrary to the drawn-out process of monarchy, our crowns come in a heavenly coronation—a celebration of Christ. We don't have to wait for a predecessor to pass away so we can rule. Jesus already did that *and* rose again. When we believe this wholeheartedly, we then have a God-given birthright to lead. And it is His royals, not the earthly ceremonies, that mark history through the way we allow Jesus to rule our lives.

If you've decided you choose Jesus over the world, you've accepted a crown not only in this life but also in the life to come.

To take on the crown is to live a life of constant persecution yet still pursue righteousness. After our first coronation is over, the hard times will come, but as long as we obey and keep our eyes on Jesus, the perfecter of our faith, we will rule effectively. In doing so, we work toward the best gift of meeting Jesus face-to-face. We also work toward this in light of our treasures in heaven.

On judgment day, we will all stand before God and "will each receive whatever we deserve for the good or evil we have done in this earthly body" (2 Cor. 5:10).

There will be negative consequences for the bad (i.e., lack of obedience/diligence). But also, *every* little thing—good deeds and divine rewards—is taken into consideration (Eph. 6:8).

We will all have rewards, but we won't all have the same prize. "He who plants and he who waters are one [in importance and esteem, working toward the same purpose]; but each will receive his own reward according to his own labor" (1 Cor. 3:8 AMP).

All of this should encourage us to do more while we reign here on earth! Do you have any ideas bursting within you? Anything at all that will bring glory to God? Then do it and do it with excellence.

Your obedience, your faith in Him, and the fruit you feed the world will determine your reward. But one thing to keep in mind is that our obedience to God is completed by His grace. It is by the fruitfulness of His own grace that He is rewarding us. Paul knew this. He said, "But whatever I am now, it is all because God poured out his special favor on me—and not without results. For I have worked harder than any of the other apostles; yet it was not I but God who was working through me by his grace" (1 Cor. 15:10).

It won't be a competition. We'll all be enthralled with His majesty and contented in His presence.

In regard to us in heaven, theologian Jonathan Edwards once said: "Though all are perfectly free from pride . . . some will have greater degrees of divine knowledge than others and will have larger capacities to see more of the divine perfections, so they will see more of their own comparative littleness and nothingness and, therefore, will be the lowest abased in humility."[3] This kind of hierarchy is one never seen before.

And so you see, our coronation is twofold. We were crowned when we accepted God's invitation to the reconciliation through Jesus, but we will also be crowned in heaven.

The Bible mentions five distinct crowns that will be placed on God's people upon entering heaven. I'll briefly list and explain them.

- *The Imperishable Crown*: awarded to those who mastered self-discipline. The Message version of 1 Corinthians 9:24–25 says, "You've all been to the stadium and seen the athletes race. Everyone runs; one wins. Run to win. All good athletes train hard. They do it for a gold medal that tarnishes and fades. You're after one that's gold eternally." In running to remain diligent, you will make a lot of sacrifices. Because you went the extra mile, God will reward you with the victor's crown for everything you gave up.
- *The Crown of Glory*: awarded to those who work in anticipation of Christ's coming. First Peter 5:4 says, "And

when the Great Shepherd appears, you will receive a crown of never-ending glory and honor." In this passage, elders were directly referred to as shepherds on earth. This suggests that those who teach and bring up God's people in the knowledge of His Word will be rewarded. This crown is also dedicated to those who proudly suffered like Christ on earth because they looked forward to the glory later to be revealed in them (Rom. 8:18).

- *The Crown of Rejoicing*: awarded to those who celebrate God's blessing of salvation. First Thessalonians 2:19 says, "After all, what gives us hope and joy, and what will be our proud reward and crown as we stand before our Lord Jesus when He returns? It is you!" When you have good news, you share it with everyone! Those who enthusiastically lead people out of the kingdom of darkness and into God's light will be rewarded. This soul winner's crown goes to those who look forward to God wiping away every tear, to those who desire to enter the place where there is no more pain (Rev. 21:4).
- *The Crown of Righteousness*: awarded to those who live righteous lives only made possible through Christ. Second Timothy 4:8 says, "Now there is in store for me the crown of righteousness, which the Lord, the righteous Judge, will award to me on that day—and not only to me, but also to all who have longed for his appearing" (NIV). This isn't self-righteousness; it is a form of godly living in which you aren't reliant on the works of your own hands. This everlasting crown awaits those who look forward to an eternity with God.

- *The Crown of Life*: awarded to every believer, but particularly to those who suffered greatly—even to the point of death. Revelation 2:10 says, "Don't be afraid of what you are about to suffer. The devil will throw some of you into prison to test you. You will suffer for ten days. But if you remain faithful even when facing death, I will give you the crown of life." Despite what the enemy throws your way, you have refuge in Jesus. This martyr's crown will be rewarded to those who love God, honor His commandments, and remain faithful in the face of tribulation.

When Queen Elizabeth II arrived at her coronation, she was adorned with a crown called the George IV State Diadem. This crown is portrayed on English stamps. Designed in 1820, the Diadem features shamrocks, roses, and thistles with 1,333 diamonds and 169 pearls.[4]

Like, whoa. If an earthly crown can be this decked out and dignified, how much more will ours be?

Surely, we can look forward to being crowned upon our arrival into heaven. And as we wait, consider: Which will you be awarded?

Thy Kingdom Come

When I first discovered that getting to heaven wasn't the only reward for living a life of obedience to God, I was super excited. I mean, who doesn't want an official crown? And one that lasts forever, at that?!

However, I didn't initially know how to explain the justification for obedience. In church, we say, "God is good, all the time," and so we believe God is good *enough*. So of course He is in heaven. Duh, Tarah-Lynn.

But if He's enough, why have rewards at all?

The best way to process this question is through the lens of Paul. You see, he was facing a dilemma—one many believers face. In a letter to the church of Philippi, he expresses how he loves being used by God, living a life of love and enthusiastically bearing fruit; however, he also longs to die and join Christ because it's "far better" than anything the world has to offer.

Later on in Philippians 3, he emphasizes how he can't wait to experience the life-giving power Christ gives now.

Um, make up your mind, Paul!

I guess he realized he would be confusing us. He goes on to explain:

> And I continually long to know the wonders of Jesus more fully and to experience the overflowing power of his resurrection working in me. I will be one with him in his sufferings and I will be one with him in his death. Only then will I be able to experience complete oneness with him in his resurrection from the realm of death. (Phil. 3:10–11 TPT)

What's this talk about resurrection? I thought we were going to live in heaven? Paul goes into more depth in the book of Romans:

> The entire universe is standing on tiptoe, yearning to see the unveiling of God's glorious sons and daughters! For against

> its will the universe itself has had to endure the empty futility resulting from the consequences of human sin. But now, with eager expectation, all creation longs for freedom from its slavery to decay and to experience with us the wonderful freedom coming to God's children. To this day we are aware of the universal agony and groaning of creation, as if it were in the contractions of labor for childbirth. And it's not just creation. We who have already experienced the firstfruits of the Spirit also inwardly groan as we passionately long to experience our full status as God's sons and daughters—including our physical bodies being transformed. (8:19–23 TPT)

Isn't that mind-blowing?

Our own resurrection will help us experience Christ fully, on a new level. When Jesus comes back, earth will be a brand-new world. It will be one that doesn't just home our spirits but one that is specifically catered to our spankin'-new bodies. This spiffy palace of an earth of ours will be perfectly suited to house God's children as well as to unveil Jesus Christ so that we may continuously enjoy Him.

Let us not get it twisted—Christ *is* enough. John Piper explains it like this: "Christ is indeed our reward, *and* everything else morally and spiritually and physically inside us and outside us in the universe—crowns, stars, cities, friends, family, great saints, etc.—everything else *with him* that will maximize the communication of his glory and our happiness in him through it."[5] We'll continue to live it up in His presence through eternal surprises. The other stuff is a bonus.

In Revelation 4:10–11, the elders in a vision exemplified this for us. Twenty-four of them fell down and worshiped the everlasting King of all kings. Laying down their crowns, they praised Him saying, "You are worthy, O Lord our God, to receive glory and honor and power. For you created all things, and they exist because you created what you pleased."

I have a question, but first, I'd like to share an integral part of the coronation ceremony with you. Before any earthly coronation begins, the archbishop must ask, "Is your Majesty ready to take the Oath?"

I'm no archbishop, but still I ask of you: Are you ready to commit to your rule?

I pray that after reading this book, your answer is yes.

As you claim your crown, may your life point people to Christ. May your whole being cry, "Thy kingdom come on earth, as it is in heaven."

Your name may not go down in history, but it'll be recorded in God's Book of Life. You will have the honor to hear, "Well done. . . . Enter into the joy of your master" (Matt. 25:23 ESV).

And we will enter into His pearly gates with gratefulness and in pure adoration, in complete awe of our precious Savior. As we give Him our best unadulterated praise, I envision us doing the same as the elders spontaneously did—laying down the very rewards given to us at His feet (Rev. 4:10). All of the titles, all of the prizes, the honors, and the possessions we may have acquired—only the best of the best—all at His feet.

Because here on earth, we claim our crowns. But in heaven, we cast them down. I can't imagine a better form of royal praise.

Acknowledgments

Mommy! You are the queen of my heart, my "mom-ager," my prayer warrior—my everything. You have allowed God to transform your pain to purpose, and I'm so honored to see your resilience, uncontained joy, and relentless faith up close. You are a blessing to anyone who has the honor of encountering your presence. So to have you as a mom? Psh. I know without a doubt that I would not be who I am without you. Thank you for teaching me how to reign confidently with my armor and my crown; I'll shine yours to sparkling perfection at every passing moment. You are the best gift a princess could ever ask for. I love you forever.

The kings of my world—Pops and my brother, Mitchie—thank you for always pushing me to be better and to never settle. Your lives are clear examples of what it means to be effective kingdom pushers. You show the world that chivalry exists, and I talk about your examples every chance I get. Thank you for encouraging me and supporting my dreams in ways I cannot even begin to count. God blessed me with an amazing family, and you two provide a great foundation. Pops, your boldness motivates me daily. And Mitch, you're my best friend. I appreciate, love, and honor you both. You will continue to conquer with grit and perseverance, and I will always be there to cheer you on, in Jesus's Name!

My first ever sissy! Medgina, thank you for being you. You're hilarious, creative, boisterous, and thoughtful, you. Thank you for always being there. Thank you for making me crack up until I cry. Thank you for reading my first drafts, helping me brainstorm, and giving me inspiration. Thank you for keeping me levelheaded, for our much-needed talks, and for being eager to celebrate my wins and uplifting me in my losses. You have helped me from shooting my book cover to debating the perfect posts for Instagram. I appreciate you for the little things and the big. You will transform the world with your boldness, your poetry, and your smile. And I can't wait to see it. I got you forever. Love you, "ceecee!!!"

My baby sister, my mini me, my forever cheerleader! Shermine, I love you. You never cease to crack me up with your wild laugh, incomparable dance moves, and our special *Hannah Montana* hugs. You are my number one fan no matter where you are in the world, and it's the sweetest thing how it never leaves your mind to share my content whether you're studying abroad or talking to friends right at home. I admire your light, enthusiasm, and heart for God (and babies). Everyone needs a Sherm in their lives. I'm so blessed to have the original.

Malissy, you were God's "surprise" blessing to me. Still can't believe how we met in college and became sisters within record time. You are a real one—someone I can cry and celebrate with—and I am overjoyed God saw fit to entrust us with a covenant friendship. I so admire your beautiful soul and will tell you how you are a gift to me and to the world with every chance I get. Thank you for always reminding me of His promises, for all of your prayers, and for seeing me through shades of beauty even when I'm feeling my lowest. I will always be there to do the same for you, and I look forward to the day the world receives healing through your angelic voice. I love you, girl!

Regine, my first ever big sister. When I was young, you instantly became someone I could look up to. It was because of your zeal for God, pure heart, and humble service to all people. It was because you were there to love on my siblings and me when my mom was in the hospital. It was because of the way you treasured and called my mom "Mom." You were always able to pray in times of heartbrokenness, encourage me when I could no longer see the light, and support me when I felt alone. I always thanked you back then, but I must publicly honor you, in this way, now. I never told you, but you were the very first person who told me that you see me writing books, working in fashion, and traveling the world. I was barely a teenager, girl! Thank you for seeing so much in me. I see the world in you. I love and appreciate you, my Banana, my bestie Sr. Lili and Sr. Mamaille, always!

Tati Yanic, my second mom—and to all of my aunts, uncles, grandmothers, and godparents, thank you for always making me your princess. I love you all so, *so* much and look forward to the day I can treasure you all like the royals you are.

Marvine, Briana, Abigael, Domonique, Sheryl, Peggy, Marge, Neph, Steph, Jenn, Helen, Woodlyne, Sheyla, Laura, Ermide,

Bianca, and all my dearest friends. I can write a book but I already did (aye)! You guys, I love you so much. You show up. Always. And that means the world. I see you and am honored to do the same in your lives.

To all of my cousins—my happiness is your happiness and your happiness is mine. I enjoy being around each and every single one of you—you all bring adventures, a world of love, and great laughs into my life. My heart explodes with love for you all in Georgia, Canada, Haiti, New York, and right here in Jersey. Thank you for holding me down!

Erline and Claudia, you are both such beautiful examples of what it means to be fierce queens and full of life. I admire your confidence and your hearts, and I am so proud to have you unapologetic boss women in my life. Thank you for taking me under your wing; I adore you both. (P.S. People, Erline's the immaculate makeup artist who slayed my look for my book cover. Louigene Artistry—book this queen!)

Pastor Feder St. Juste, Pastor Pierrot, the Josiases, the Sauveurs, Sister Solange, Brother Cadet, Brother Bond, Brother Jimmy, and my Bethany family! Thank you for seeing so much in me and for me. I appreciate your push to use my gifts, your trust in me to lead our youth, and your powerful prayers for me and my family. Pastor Feder, I especially thank you for always being one phone call away—your huge heart does not go unnoticed! Sister Ruth and Fr. Wilbens, thank you for your constant encouragement and for lovingly welcoming us into your home for amazing food and fellowship. May God bless all of your families!

My beautiful Bethany, thank you for giving me my own princess! I'm already having so much fun dressing up little Rebekah.

I am honored to be her godmother. I really can't wait to help guide her and Tabby into becoming the women of God they are destined to be. Love you and your precious family so much.

My agent, Tim Beals, thank you for answering my email! I had no idea what I was doing but you saw God at work. Thank you for investing in me and showing me how this book industry operates! I am grateful for all you do.

My Baker/Revell team. Thank you for believing in me so much you decided to stick with me for three! I appreciate your keen insight and ongoing support in bringing my stories to life. Kelsey, you've shown me the ropes throughout this process, and I'm so grateful that you support my mission. I am thankful for your wit, your feedback, and how you are always cheering me on. You're awesome, girl.

Kathy Magrino, for giving me the college assignment to begin a blog. Who would've known it would lead me to here! Thank you for supporting me since day one.

To my *Adorned in Armor* and *Dressed for Battle* families and my precious readers—thank you for supporting me in every adventure. I am honored to be your sister.

Notes

Chapter 1 A Royal Reality

1. Mathew Jedeikin, "One Small Detail about Cinderella, Belle, and Tiana That Will Blow Your Mind," BuzzFeed, February 2, 2016, accessed June 25, 2018, https://www.buzzfeed.com/mathewjedeikin/all-three-disney-princesses-by-marriage-wore-gloves.

Chapter 4 Abdication

1. "Impeachment," US House of Representatives: History, Art & Archives, accessed June 25, 2018, https://history.house.gov/Institution/Origins-Development/Impeachment/.

Chapter 5 Fairest of Them All

1. Jacob Grimm, Wilhelm Grimm, Peter Carter, and Rosamund Fowler, *Fairy Tales from Grimm* (Oxford: Oxford University Press, 1982), 238.

2. Jon Bloom, "You Are God's Workmanship," Desiring God, May 11, 2015, accessed January 26, 2019, https://www.desiringgod.org/articles/you-are-gods-workmanship.

3. John Piper, "Women the World Cannot Explain," Desiring God, September 18, 2015, accessed January 26, 2019, https://www.desiringgod.org/messages/women-the-world-cannot-explain.

4. "Kosmos—The NAS New Testament Greek Lexicon," Bible Study Tools, accessed January 27, 2019, https://www.biblestudytools.com/lexicons/greek/nas/kosmos.html.

5. Amanda Criss, "The Fourfold Beauty of a Godly Woman," DesiringGod.org, May 5, 2016, accessed January 26, 2019, https://www.desiringgod.org/articles/the-fourfold-beauty-of-a-godly-woman.

6. Mike Bickle, "The Power of Delighting in God's Beauty," *International House of Prayer* (blog)," January 26, 2017, accessed January 26, 2019, https://www.ihopkc.org/resources/blog/power-delighting-gods-beauty/.

Chapter 6 The Royal Treatment

1. Steven Furtick, "Walking in the Favor of God," Inspiration Ministries, accessed July 25, 2018, https://inspiration.org/christian-articles/walking-in-the-favor-of-god/.

2. "Intro to Esther," The International Bible Society, October 8, 2016, accessed December 2018, https://www.biblica.com/resources/scholar-notes/niv-study-bible/intro-to-esther/.

3. Tarah-Lynn Saint-Elien, "Reconnecting with My Haitian Roots at the PapJazz Festival," *Teen Vogue*, March 29, 2018, https://www.teenvogue.com/story/haiti-papjazz-festival-review-shithole-country-trump.

Chapter 7 The Royal Brigade

1. Elise Taylor, "Prince George, Queen Elizabeth, and the Scary Issue of Royal Security," *Vogue*, September 15, 2017, accessed February 25, 2019, https://www.vogue.com/article/prince-george-queen-elizabeth-royal-security.

2. Eric Milzarski, "6 Well-Known Ways the White House Stays Secure," We Are The Mighty, July 23, 2018, accessed December 8, 2018, https://www.wearethemighty.com/history/white-house-security-measures?rebelltitem=7#rebelltitem7.

3. Tyler Rogoway, "The Fascinating Anatomy of the Presidential Motorcade," The Drive, July 22, 2016, accessed December 8, 2018, http://thedrive.com/the-war-zone/4518/the-fascinating-anatomy-of-the-presidential-motorcade.

Chapter 9 Bow Down

1. Maria Bobila, "The Saint Laurent Heart Coat: A Love Story," Fashionista, October 7, 2016, accessed December 25, 2018, https://fashionista.com/2016/10/ysl-heart-coat.

2. C. S. Lewis, *Mere Christianity* (New York: Walker & Co., 1987), chap. 8.

3. R. C. Sproul, "Christian Humility," Ligonier Ministries, accessed December 26, 2018, https://www.ligonier.org/learn/devotionals/christian-humility/.

4. Nellie Owens, "Humility: What the Bible Really Says about Being Humble," Active Christianity, November 5, 2018, accessed December 26, 2019, https://activechristianity.org/4-things-everyone-should-know-about-humility.

5. John Piper, "Blessed Are the Meek," DesiringGod.org, February 9, 1986, accessed December 26, 2018, https://www.desiringgod.org/messages/blessed-are-the-meek.

Chapter 10 Check Your Court

1. "Lady in Waiting," Elizabethan-Era.org, accessed December 26, 2018, http://www.elizabethan-era.org.uk/lady-in-waiting.htm.

2. Christine Hoover, *Messy Beautiful Friendship: Finding and Nurturing Deep and Lasting Relationships* (Grand Rapids: Baker Books, 2017), 27–28.

3. Hoover, *Messy Beautiful Friendship*, 29.

4. "The Heather Lindsey Show: What Is a Godly Friendship?," YouTube, 8:48, May 18, 2017, https://youtu.be/KXf9v_DNQsw.

5. Matthew Stevenson, All Nations Chicago, "6 Ministries of the Family," YouTube, November 19, 2018, accessed January 26, 2019, https://www.youtube.com/watch?v=ZkJt76v-Wb0.

6. Rachel Lehner, "12 Characteristics of Christian Friendship," Unlocking the Bible, September 16, 2016, accessed January 26, 2019, https://unlockingthebible.org/2016/09/12-characteristics-of-christian-friendship/.

Chapter 11 Secure Your Palace

1. "A Jealous God," All About God, accessed January 26, 2019, https://www.allaboutgod.com/a-jealous-god.htm.

2. Richard L. Strauss, "A Jealous God," Bible.org, accessed January 26, 2019, https://bible.org/seriespage/jealous-god.

3. John Piper, "Fear and Hope in God's Jealousy," Desiring God, September 19, 2019, https://www.desiringgod.org/articles/fear-and-hope-in-gods-jealousy.

Chapter 15 A Purpose-Filled Reign

1. Talia Lakritz, "Here's What the Royal Family Does When They Receive an Official Gift," INSIDER, January 18, 2018, accessed February 8, 2019, https://www.thisisinsider.com/royal-family-gifts-2018-1.

Chapter 16 Queen of Hearts

1. Robin Gallaher Branch, "Tabitha in the Bible," Biblical Archaeology Society, April 27, 2016, accessed January 26, 2019, https://www.biblicalarchaeology.org/daily/people-cultures-in-the-bible/people-in-the-bible/tabitha-in-the-bible/.

2. Laurel Meyer, "Tabitha: A Woman God Used (Acts 9:36–43)," Tomorrow's World, January 6, 2016, accessed January 27, 2019, https://www.tomorrowsworld.org/woman-to-woman/tabitha-a-woman-god-used-acts-9 36-43.

Chapter 17 You Are Seen

1. DeNeen L. Brown, "How Aretha Franklin's 'Respect' Became an Anthem for Civil Rights and Feminism," *Washington Post*, August 16, 2018, accessed February 9, 2019, https://www.washingtonpost.com/news/retropolis/wp/20

18/08/14/how-aretha-franklins-respect-became-an-anthem-for-civil-rights-and-feminism/?utm_term=.34ba58965f32.

2. "Phebe, Phoebe: The Woman Who Wore the Badge of Kindness," Biblegateway.com, accessed February 10, 2019, https://www.biblegateway.com/resources/all-women-bible/Phebe-Phoebe.

3. Florence Taylor, "Sister, Servant and Leader: Who Was Phoebe in the Bible?," *Christianity Today*, July 4, 2016, https://www.christiantoday.com/article/sister-servant-and-leader-who-was-phoebe-in-the-bible/89442.htm.

Chapter 18 Treasure

1. John Piper, "Is Online Dating Good for Christians?," Desiring God, August 12, 2014, accessed January 20, 2019, https://www.desiringgod.org/interviews/is-online-dating-good-for-christians.

Chapter 19 Dressed for Battle

1. "What Does It Mean That Jesus Is the Prince of Peace (Isaiah 9:6)?," Got Questions, November 19, 2010, accessed January 26, 2019, https://www.gotquestions.org/Prince-of-Peace.html.

2. Havilah Cunnington, *Stronger than the Struggle: Uncomplicating Your Spiritual Battle* (Nashville: Nelson, 2018), 142.

Chapter 20 Defending Honor

1. Billy Graham, "A Classic Billy Graham Message: In the World, But Not of It," Billy Graham Evangelistic Association, January 28, 2016, accessed January 26, 2019, https://billygraham.org/decision-magazine/february-2016/a-classic-billy-graham-message-in-the-world-but-not-of-it/.

2. Merriam-Webster.com, s.v. "chivalry," accessed February 10, 2019, https://www.merriam-webster.com/dictionary/chivalry.

3. Simon Newman, "Chivalry in the Middle Ages," The Finer Times, accessed February 14, 2019, http://www.thefinertimes.com/Middle-Ages/chivalry-in-the-middle-ages.html.

4. Matthew Stevenson, "Mystery of Consecration—Apostle Matthew Stevenson," YouTube, August 30, 2012, accessed February 12, 2019, https://www.youtube.com/watch?v=8pTYCyCxZyE.

5. Stevenson, "Mystery of Consecration."

Chapter 21 Coronation Day

1. "50 Facts about the Queen's Coronation," The Royal Family, June 7, 2017, accessed January 24, 2019, https://www.royal.uk/50-facts-about-queens-coronation-0.

2. "Coronation of the British Monarch," Revolvy, accessed January 20, 2019, https://www.revolvy.com/page/Coronation-of-the-British-monarch.

3. Jonathan Edwards, "Heaven, a World of Love," Biblebb.com, accessed February 1, 2019, http://www.biblebb.com/files/edwards/charity16.htm.

4. "50 Facts about the Queen's Coronation."

5. John Piper, "What's the Appeal of Heavenly Rewards Other Than Getting Christ?," Desiring God, March 27, 2017, emphasis added, accessed February 26, 2019, https://www.desiringgod.org/interviews/whats-the-appeal-of-heavenly-rewards-other-than-getting-christ.

Tarah-Lynn Saint-Elien is a fierce and favored fashionista, encouraging and equipping thousands of women to fully grasp their worth in Christ through her award-winning brand, Adorned in Armor. By landing internships at *Elle* magazine and PBS, and by collaborating with brands such as Maybelline and Banana Republic, she has been catapulted into becoming a *Teen Vogue* "It Girl" and later a *Teen Vogue* fashion writer. Crowned Miss Black New Jersey in 2018, Tarah-Lynn graduated summa cum laude from Rider University and earned her master's degree from Syracuse University. The Haitian-American beauty queen hosts the *Dressed for Battle* podcast, contributes to the *Haitian Times*, and can run in heels like it's nobody's business! Tarah-Lynn loves to travel and is available to book for your event. For more, follow @adornedinarmor or head over to adornedinarmor.com.

Connect with Tarah

ADORNED *in* ARMOR

Dressed for Battle

AdornedInArmor.com